SUSTAINABLE COMPUTER ENVIRONMENTS

CULTURES OF SUPPORT IN ENGLISH STUDIES AND LANGUAGE ARTS

NEW DIMENSIONS IN COMPUTERS AND COMPOSITION

Gail E. Hawisher and Cynthia L. Selfe, editors

Sustainable Computer Environments: Cultures of Support in English
Studies and Language Arts
Richard Selfe

Doing Literacy Online: Teaching, Learning, and Playing
in an Electronic World
Ilana Snyder and Catherine Beavis (eds.)

forthcoming

Digital Youth: Technologies and the Future of Literacy
Jonathan Alexander

Role Play: Distance Learning and the Teaching of Writing
Jonathan Alexander and Marcia Dickson (eds.)

Lingua Franca: Towards a Rhetoric of New Media
Colin Brooke

Aging Literacies: Training and Development Challenges for Faculty
Angela Crow

Datacloud: Toward a New Theory of Online Work
Johndan Johnson-Eilola

At Play in the Fields of Writing: A Serio-Ludic Rhetoric
Albert Rouzie

Labor, Writing Technologies and the Shaping of Composition
in the Academy
Pamela Takayoshi and Patricia Sullivan (eds.)

Integrating Hypertextual Subjects: Computers, Composition, Critical
Literacy and Academic Labor
Robert Samuels

SUSTAINABLE COMPUTER ENVIRONMENTS

CULTURES OF SUPPORT IN ENGLISH STUDIES AND LANGUAGE ARTS

Richard Selfe

Michigan Technology University

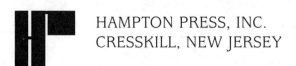

HAMPTON PRESS, INC.
CRESSKILL, NEW JERSEY

Printed in the United States of America

Library of Congress Cataloging-in-Publication Data

Selfe, Richard.
   Sustainable computer environments : cultures of support in English studies and language arts / Richard Selfe.
      p. cm. -- (New dimensions in computers and composition)
   Includes bibliographical references and index.
   ISBN 1-57273-586-4 -- ISBN 1-57273-587-2
      1. English philology--Computer-assisted instruction. 2. English philology--Study and teaching--Data processing. 3. English philology--Study and teaching--Technological innovations. 4. Language arts--Computer-assisted instruction. 5. Educational technology. I. Title. II. Series.

   PE66.S47 2004
   428'.0078'5--dc22

                                          2004054237

Hampton Press, Inc.
23 Broadway
Cresskill, NJ 07626

CONTENTS

Preface   ix
Acknowledgments   xxi

1   The Related Challenges of Digital Literacy and the Dynamic of Blame   1

Summary of Topics   1
The Link Between Literacy and Computers is Forged   2
The Role of English and Language Arts Teachers   7
The Dynamic of Blame   8
People, First; Pedagogy, Second; and Technology, Third   12
Some Challenges to This Planning Process   13

2   Establishing a Culture of Support Within Which Teachers Come First, Pedagogy Second, and Technology Third   23

Summary of Topics   23
Moving Away From the Dynamic of Blame and Toward a Culture of Support   24
Successful Cultures of Support   41
Chapter Conclusion   49

3   Planning Technology-Rich Environments   53

Summary of Topics   53
Working With Heart, as Well as Head and Hands   54
Reflections on a Cyborg Environment   56
A Brief Case Study: Valuing Collaboration Through User-Centered Design   74
Conclusion: On a Stakeholder-Centered Design Process   76
A Summary and the Following Chapters   82

v

4 Making Systems Work in Sustainable Ways: Student Technology Assistants and Effective Fiscal Models 85

Summary of Topics   85
Student Workers at the Center of Things   86
An Argument for Involving Students   87
A Case Study: From Goals to Sustainable Student-Centered
  Technology Environments   87
More Arguments for Involving Students   90
Creating Student Technology Assistant (STA) Programs   92
Talking to Teachers With Experience: STA Programs   97
Creating a Sustainable Budget and Fiscal System   105
The Entrepreneurial Model   110
The Grant Funding Model   115
The Student Lab Fee Model   117
The Central Computer Funding Model   118
Conclusion   119

5 Assessing and Redesigning Sustainable Computer Efforts 121

Summary of Topics   121
Three Assumptions About Assessment   123
A Model of Assessment and Redesign   124
Step 1: Identify Stakeholders   126
Step 2; Define Issues and Areas on Which to Focus   131
Step 3; Identify Specific Sites of Effort and Involvement   133
Step 4: Identify Sites for Increased Involvement and
  Investment   136
Step 5; Pinpoint and Fine-Tune Involvement   141
Why Such a Complex Effort?   146

Afterword: Final Summary and Comments   149

Appendixes

2.1: Techno-Pedagogical Explorations: Toward Sustainable
    Technology-Rich Instruction   153
4.1: The Economy of the CCLI   165
5.1: *Access* Redefined   171
5.2: Teaching with Information Technology (TWIT)   177

References   179
Author Index   183
Subject Index   185

List of Figures

1.1   A Dynamic of Blame   10
3.1   A List of Student Literacy Needs Compiled by One of the English/Language Arts Teachers   61
3.2   Instructional Goals for MTU's CCLI   63
3.3   Operational Goalds for Michigan Tech's CCLI   68
5.1   Assessment & Redesign Matrix, Version 1: Levels of involvement in the technology-rich environments of the Humanities Department at MTU   *Insert*
5.2   Three Versions of the Assessment and Redesign Matrix   125
5.3   Identifying Current Sites of Effort and Involvement in the Cells of the Assessment/Redesign Matrix, Version 1   134
5.4   Assessment & Redesign Matrix, Version 2: A plan for improved involvement in the TR environments in the Humanities Department at MTU   *Insert*
5.5   Assessment & Redesign Matrix, Version 3: Moments of intervention in the issues of technology-rich environments   *Insert*
5.6   Identifying Tactical Moments for Involvement in Technological Projects   144-145

List of Tables

5.1   General Categories of Budgetary Expenditures as Estimated by Workers in Computer-Rich English and Language Arts Facilities   108

PREFACE

SUMMARY OF TOPICS

▶ Audiences & justifications (p. x)
▶ An activist mentality (p. xiii)
▶ English teachers as technology activists (p. xviii)
▶ An overview (p. xx)

This is a book for teachers of English studies, technical or professional communication, composition, and language arts (K–college)[1] who use—or want to use—communication technologies in their classes and support their use locally. It is a book, as well, for those administrators and staff members responsible for helping to support and sustain such instructional efforts. Its purpose, simply put, is to describe how to create a robust, sus-

---

[1] I use the general phrase English studies and language arts to refer to a wide collection of educational disciplines (later I abbreviate it further by referring to English and language arts. At the college level, these include teachers, administrators, and technical professionals who teach or support composition, technical or professional communication, English as a second language (ESL), literature, rhetoric, and new media classes, among others. In the K–12 arena, it includes any class that has a substantial communication component at some point in the year. In fact the workshops mentioned in the last chapter of this volume are often based on communication efforts across the curriculum in K-12 and college. Teachers, administrators, and professionals who are interested in technology-enriched language and communicative arts curricula will find this book of special interest.

tainable system of support for technology-rich teaching and learning efforts—an infrastructure that supports innovation in teaching literacy practices, based on the commitment of multiple stakeholders. It concludes by emphasizing an ongoing assessment and redesign process that promotes productive change over time in technology-rich environments (physical and online).

Even in this dynamic technological age, when computers and related technologies have become exponentially more sophisticated with each new generation of hardware and software, computer-supported instructional efforts can be difficult to get underway. All too often, such efforts are short-lived—they fail the test of time, at least partly, because of the instability inherent in computer technology. The technological systems on which computer-supported instructional efforts depend change with remarkable and often damaging rapidity. Specifically, because these systems continue to change, computer-supported instructional efforts can fail because they prove to be a continuous drain on programmatic and departmental resources: human and fiscal.

As I said elsewhere, all technology-rich instruction[2] is exploratory (Selfe, "Techno-pedagogical"). These instructional efforts are difficult to sustain because they require ongoing professional development programs and a commitment to innovation. They require constant monitoring of students' literacy needs and skills. Teachers, administrators, and staff members must engage in continuous learning, experimentation, and formative assessment on top of their traditional duties. Often the leaders of technology-rich programs—teachers, administrators, and staff members—need different kinds of support at different points in time and in their careers. If we acknowledge the fluid nature of technology-rich instructional environments and efforts, it should not surprise us that some explorations are short-lived.

However, integrating technology-rich instruction in English studies and the language arts curricula is not a hopeless task. It is complex and requires constant vigilance, but there are many success stories. Throughout the book, generous colleagues have contributed specific examples of *sustainable practices* that have been developed at their colleges and K–12 institutions. These examples represent specific contextualized projects, programs, and approaches that illustrate the generalized arguments made in this volume.

---

[2]You will notice that I interchange the phrases computer-supported and technology-rich throughout the book. I do this for stylistic reasons even though I am aware that they are not perfectly parallel descriptions.

Extrapolating from these local practices, readers can imagine how they might implement or agitate for similar approaches in their own programs, schools, and institutions. The references and contact information in each sustainable practice should be useful as readers plan and implement sustainable institutional or classroom-specific practices of their own.

Given the challenges that computer-supported instructional efforts face, it is clear that sustainable practices (not short-term solutions) are essential to the successful integration of technologies into English, language arts, and literacy instruction. This fact is as true for a rural elementary school in Michigan that wants to support elementary language arts teachers who use online learning circles as it is for a consortium of Ivy League universities that want to support faculty who are building a multimedia environment in which to teach the works of William Blake. Computer-using teachers need robust, connected, electronic teaching environments that allow for a wide range of teaching styles and learning efforts, in multiple media, and over a sustained period of time.

This volume suggests that English and language arts teachers can—and indeed should—develop an open and systematic approach to creating and maintaining the infrastructure needed for technology-rich literacy instruction. My interest in this type of study is based, for the most part, on three kinds of input. First, on information obtained from a survey of 191 individuals in 55 computer-using English departments around the country, each of whom described the efforts that worked well to support online teaching and learning and those that worked less effectively (cf. Selfe, D. Institutional). Second, I rely on my experience over the last 17 years conducting technology workshops with K-college teachers and administrators at MTU and at other institutions.[3] Finally, I am of course influenced and inspired by the set of sustainable practices in this book—examples of successful computer-supported instructional programs found in language arts and English studies departments around the country. They provide examples of just a few of the creative ways in which teachers, administrators, staff members, and student workers have learned to cope with the current situation and even to thrive on our techno-pedagogical challenges.

The survey, published in 1998, illustrates the creative but haphazard way in which many institutions were supporting—or failing to support—computer-rich instruction in the last decade of the 20th century. Unfortunately, my other, more recent experiences have convinced me that

---

[3]For recent iterations of these two-week summer institutes, check these Web sites: http://www.hu.mtu.edu/ciwic and http://www.hu.mtu.edu/ecac.

things have not changed substantially over the past 5 years. For 17 years, teachers attending MTU's Computers in Writing-Intensive Classrooms and workshops I have conducted at other institutions have continued to provide anecdotes about haphazard support and unsustainable efforts. Both the survey and anecdotal information indicate that few English and language arts programs attend carefully to the entire range of human, financial, technical, and even policy-level infrastructures that influence the innovative instructional efforts of computer-using teachers. Such tunnel vision, as Brown and Duguid (2000) suggest in their book *The Social Life of Information*, is symptomatic of our culture, not just literacy professionals. They suggest that,

> this central focus [what they call "tunnel design"] inevitably pushes aside all the fuzzy stuff that lies around the edges [of technological systems]—context, background, history, common knowledge, social resources. But this stuff around the edges is not as irrelevant as it may seem. It provides valuable balance and perspective. (p. 1)

They refer to balancing the system- or technology-centered discussions that often dominate educational technology decision making. I would suggest further that understanding the "fuzzy stuff," or what could be called *institutional infrastructure*, not only adds balance and perspective, but makes it possible to develop sustainable, usable, and appropriate technology-rich instructional systems.

Is there any reason to think that educators are now finding it easier to create the complex infrastructures that support computer-using teachers? Unfortunately, the ubiquitous nature of computing means that such infrastructures are receding even further into the background of our attention. Although increasing numbers of departments, teachers, and administrators are concerned about the impact of technology, the infrastructure that supports such systems seems more complex and impenetrable than ever, and most departments and institutions continue to struggle to understand what is needed to support and assess computer-supported teaching and learning efforts. This situation leaves most teachers in a poor position to be technological activists: not technological advocates, but local, informed, critical activists as described in the final chapter of this book.

As things stand, then, teachers—even some of those who are most enthusiastic about technology's promise—feel disenfranchised from the process of making technology policy in their programs, departments, and schools and believe they can have little or no influence on the larger technological systems that are changing dynamically the world and their own profession. In other words, some of the most innovative teachers (and students) in schools are set up to be end-of-the-pipe consumers of technological systems, but are not given the resources they need to influence or shape these systems even as those same systems are constantly being redesigned within our schools. This book is intended to give interested English and language arts teachers, administrators, students, and technicians a sense of agency—to encourage them to become technological activists who are willing to productively influence and shape the technological systems around them.

To encourage an activist mentality, this book provides specific descriptions of programs that have established successful environments for computer-using teachers of English studies and the communicative arts—descriptions written by faculty, administrators, and staff members from a wide range of institutions around the country. In these descriptions, readers will find cultures of support that not only encourage teachers to use computers, but also help them actively shape computer environments in their K–college institutions. The descriptions challenge our imaginations by suggesting methods for sustaining professional development efforts; suggesting how to collaborate with a range of individuals to design and operate technology-rich labs, classrooms, and virtual systems; suggesting how to involve students and administrators, as well as faculty and staff in assessing the success of computer-supported communication; and suggesting how to build a core of student support staff who provide the desk-side attention that teachers need.

The first of these sustainable practices comes from Ball State University. It illustrates their philosophy behind a rhetorically based faculty development process that involves many of the characteristics of what I call, in chapter 2, a culture of support. The second sustainable practice comes from BreadNet, a literature-based graduate program for K-12 teachers of English and language arts. This program involves classroom teachers in summer study at a common onsite location at Middlebury College in Middlebury Vermont, but it also supports their efforts throughout the year with a networked computer system.

Rhetorical Faculty Development: Reflection, Reflexion, and Action

Carole Clark Papper and Rich Rice, Ball State University

The Ball State example here illustrates how important it is to apply a multifaceted approach to faculty development efforts that are sustained over time. There practices are important because they illustrate a culture of support that recognizes the cyclical nature of professional development: new teachers come into the system, older teachers become interested, technologies and administrative planning changes, funding models get revised, ... One has to have a philosophy that makes it possible to reimagine technology-rich instruction as the ground changes under your feet (*Dickie Selfe*).

Effective learning is wholehearted, sincere, and responsible, and can develop into lifelong learning by teaching students how to be reflective, reflexive, and active. Reflection is the close, ongoing consideration of a subject. Reflexivity involves dialectically engaging with that subject from multiple perspectives. After discovering and arranging ideas, learners can put them into action. This process is a useful cycle for faculty development as well.

The Ball State University English Department has been using this model for several years. We begin with an idea or epiphany and assess available resources; we consider people's needs and goals; we devise a strategy to honestly assess our progress, and then we look for opportunities to apply what we've learned. Faculty interest remains high when this cycle is reapplied in different contexts.

We began from the premise that if our teachers were to meet the needs of students facing a world increasingly oriented toward and shaped by computer technology, those teachers needed to embrace the computer as more than "just another pedagogical tool." To create an atmosphere where committed teachers could explore various technologies in supportive environments, we determined the resources we needed and wrote successful grants. The grants provided funding for faculty training, including intensive 2-week summer workshops, day-long seminars during the school year, one-on-one "kairotic" consulting, and periodic "Best Practice" showcases. We reassessed our needs, however, and the Writing, Computers, and Literacy Initiative (WCLI) was born. This grant provided additional computer-mediated teaching and learning resources, leading us to a new understanding and practice of literacy in our department.

Still many incoming students were having difficulty learning writing in our computer environments. In thinking through this, building on our successful workshop, and consulting experiences, we decided to adapt models like The Epiphany Project(http://) and the MTU Computers in Writing-Intensive Classrooms institute (http://www.hu.mtu.edu/~ciwic) to our local context. We created the Pedagogy, Practice, and Technology of Writing Institute (PPTW) for Indiana K-16 teachers. In this 4-day, intensive summer program, we explore how to use computers to teach writing, from word-processing to synchronous and asynchronous exchange, from creating syllawebs to electronic portfolios. Our training is based on the resources teachers have access to in their own schools. We explore teaching and learning resources on the World Wide Web, including building Web pages, and we investigate presentation technologies and hypertext writing tools. Through getting involved in this program, many of our teachers became immersed in a larger community as well: the field of computers and writing. We reassessed what we learned through WCLI and PPTW, and we decided to host the Computers and Writing Conference (CW2001). The theme for the conference was central to what we continue to come back to in our own faculty development: "how might teacher-scholars map the progress of technology in our reading and writing classrooms?" By reassessing our needs using reflection, reflexivity, and action in different contexts—departmental, institutional, local community, larger community—we continue to maintain the interest of our faculty to build strong teaching praxis.

More about WCLI, PPTW, CW2001, and this faculty development model can be found through http://english.ttu.edu/kairos/5.2/binder.html?coverweb/Papperreynoldsrice.

BreadNet and the Bread Loaf School of English

Chris Benson & Rocky Gooch, BreadNet

This best practice illustrates how a literature-based program that offers Graduate K–12 English master's degrees is supported by conti nous electronic collaborations through the year on a network systems called BreadNet. It incorporates four widely dispersed campuses and encourages discussions between teachers and students across cultural topics. These are real audiences talking about real issues that count as important to the teachers and students participating. Their support system includes face-to-face, on-the-spot tutorials of increasing complexity during summer sessions, but also provides visiting staff during the year.

BreadNet is a FirstClass communications software [a commercial program] used by the Bread Loaf School of English, Middlebury College, to link over 200 teachers (primarily middle and high school English teachers) who are avid users of technology to create networked learning across distance, time, age, and cultures. The Bread Loaf School of English (BLSE) has existed since 1921 as a 6-week summer graduate program. Students there are typically teachers of English, and the program requires five summers of residence to complete. Electronic networking enables teachers in the program to continue with collaborations they begin during their summers of residency together. BreadNet originated in 1984 and has undergone several user interfaces before arriving at the current, user-friendly format of FirstClass software. As computer conferencing capabilities of BreadNet have improved, the school has grown, comprising four summer campus: Middlebury College, VT; Lincoln College, Oxford, England; Institute of American Indian Arts, Santa Fe, NM; and University of Alaska, Juneau. Linking over 400 far-flung students who hail from all parts of the United States and many parts of the world becomes a daunting task, but BreadNet has served to establish electronic connections among these teachers who use the service to network learning projects among students from various places.

The ability to network learning among various students raises issues associated with cross-cultural curricula, and BreadNet has been a catalyst for teachers to explore controversial subjects with different kinds of students. Many [online] conferences are focused around shared reading of literature that raises such issues for students, For example,

- Students in an expensive, elite, private boarding school in New England discussed African-American and African poetry with middle- class students of Nairobi, Kenya.
- Native American and Native Alaskan students from various tribes, including Zuni, Navajo, Inupiat, and Yu'pik, connected online to discuss the benefits and compromises experiences in living in "two worlds," the native world and that of mainstream America.
- Students in Ketchikan, AK, and Chinle, AZ, read literature related to youth gang and collaborated on plans to rid their communities of gang activtities.

These few examples show the controversial subjects that are brought to the fore when students from different cultures begin to speak to each other about issues raised in their curricula. Students write on BreadNet for real audiences, and this gives them a deeper and broader experience in the complex process of communicating, far more complex than the typical writing classroom of yesterday when students wrote themes primarily for the teacher's eyes only.

A second use of BreadNet is teacher-to-teacher communication. Our country has never been in such an upheaval over issues of public education, from the standards movement to racial prejudice in schools to school violence to inequity in school funding. BLSE teachers are eager to learn all they can about these and other issues from each other. Each of these subjects has been the focus of substantive and sustained discussions among teachers, many of whom call the teacher-to-teacher discussions a "lifeline," especially those teachers in very rural and remote locations.

After 15 years of networking teachers with BreadNet, we know that support must be ongoing and varied to meet teachers' varied needs. One-shot tutorials don't work, and one size doesn't fit all. When teachers attend a Bread Loaf campus, they are provided with BreadNet accounts and free software and invited to use the system. Those attending on fellowships are required to learn and use BreadNet. A computer center staffed with several assistants provides on-the-spot tutorials all summer long. As Bread Loaf is a 6-week summer program, these tutorials can be done numerous times, increasing in complexity as a student progresses. By the end of the 6-week program, even the most stalwart technophobe is able to use the system with some ease. BLSE maintains a very small staff during the regular academic year to troubleshoot problems that users encounter. Some staff regularly hit the road as often as twice a month on tours of schools in far-flung places where they provide technical assistance to teachers in their classrooms and homes or consult with technology leaders in the teachers' schools.

For more information about BreadNet, go to <http://www.blse.middlebury.edu/blsefiles/BLSEBnet.html>.

ENGLISH TEACHERS AS TECHNOLOGY ACTIVISTS

I end this Preface with a few words about the readers for whom this book will be most useful and some of the theorists who inform the many practical chapters to follow. My background in technical communication and commitment to user-centered design (articulated in a useful way by Robert Johnson in *User-Centered Technology: A Rhetorical Theory for Computers and Other Mundane Artifacts*) encourages me to look for a range of stakeholders in any complex endeavor. To create and sustain the infrastructure needed for successful computer-rich programs in English studies and the language arts, we have to consider involving more teachers than those few individuals who commit early and enthusiastically to computer technology. We also need to think about involving teachers who take on computer-supported instructional efforts later in the game; administrators of programs that use computer technology; staff members who run the technological systems on which English and language arts programs depend; and, most important, the students who use and often help maintain these systems.

Perhaps the most important reason for all of these individuals to explore the potential of computers in programs that support literacy instruction grows out of an understanding that technological systems are both *overdetemined* (cf. Feenberg, 1991) and *underdetermined* (cf. Feenberg, 1995). Such systems are overdetermined because powerful social, governmental, and financial forces are at work to shape the ways we interact with computers. For instance, our culture's growing economic dependence on technology exports and the increasing uses of technology in the public sphere help convince parents and educators that youngsters have a better chance of succeeding in highly valued workplaces if they have a high-tech education. The effects of such factors are magnified when professional organizations like the NCTE issue standards that define literacy, in part, as the ability to "use a variety of technological and informational resources (e.g., libraries, databases, computer networks, video) to gather and synthesize information and to create and communicate knowledge" (p. 39), and when state boards of education follow suit with similar standards that affect English and language arts curricula more directly and on more local levels (chap. 1 details these efforts more thoroughly).

Adding to the tendential force generated by these combined factors is the funding that the federal government and the various states provide for schools willing to integrate computers into their curricula. Working in concert with this already complex constellation of forces are the pressures exerted by a growing computer industry that offers high-paying jobs to high-tech graduates, parents working in high-tech industries who want the best education for their children, school principals who must demonstrate that their schools are keeping up with the times, and students who are already used to conducting literacy practices in computer-supported environments as they enter our schools. Together these factors (and others) constitute an impressive array of forces at work to overdetermine the actions of teachers and the direction and shape of computer-supported instruction in English and language arts classrooms.

Yet, technological systems—like those characterizing most English language arts programs and departments—are also *underdetermined* in important ways. For instance, despite the many sociocultural forces exerting pressure on educators to integrate technology into curricula, most literacy professionals have some discretion in determining if and when technology should be used in their own classrooms. They also have the responsibility and expertise to shape how computers should be employed. Similarly, computer-supported communication facilities—labs, writing centers, literacy centers—provide landscapes in which computer-supported English and language arts teachers, administrators, and staff members can assume some level of control over technology—even as these spaces and systems change on a continual basis. Within such landscapes, students can learn how to use language effectively in online environments to shape their world; teachers can learn how to exert collective consumer and tactical pressures on the companies that manufacture computer software and hardware; and administrators can learn how to formulate productive technology policies that are inclusive.

"In the digital world many of the distinctions between designers and users are becoming blurred. We are all, to some extent, designers now" (Brown & Duguid, p. 4). This statement represents both the promise and challenge of technology—not that *technology* will make a difference, but that, working from a humanistic understanding of technology, teachers of English and language arts can make that difference. We can be both designers and users of the digital world.

Specifically, this book provides practical advice for teachers and other stakeholders who want to take part in creating a productive culture of support for the technology-rich teaching of literacy skills and values. The chapters that follow describe how teachers—working collaboratively with administrators, staff, and students—can create the following elements of such an environment:

- an ongoing commitment to technological activism that can help departments move away from a dynamic of blame toward a more productive culture of support—one that maintains a priority, first, on people and their language needs; second, on teaching and instructional goals; and, finally, on the thoughtful and critical use of technology (chaps. 1 & 2);
- a planning process that helps sustain computer-supported communication environments so that teachers can provide robust learning experiences for students over time (chap. 3);
- a team of stakeholders (including student workers) who recognize the growing importance of technological literacy in an increasingly global culture and who have a personal interest in creating a culture of support that can sustain technology-rich teaching of literacy values and skills over the long term (chap. 4);
- a process of budgeting for technology that supports systematic planning, maintenance, and replacement of equipment (chap. 4);
- an ongoing program of formative assessment and re-design that will help guide departmental efforts to support the technology-rich environments that we are always in the process of creating or re-invigorating (chap. 5).

ACKNOWLEDGMENTS

There would be no book, no interest on my part in student technological literacy practices, no effort to begin a dialogue about sustainable technological environments, no concern about these cyborg entities that we have all become so accustomed to and dependent upon without the persistent and thoughtful help of several groups and individuals. First, even though it was so very long ago, I must thank my dissertation committee at MTU for being willing to read in such a tangential area and for encouraging me to complete a dissertation that, in most peoples' eyes, would be outside the scope of a Humanities department. Those extremely helpful individuals were Drs. Marilyn Cooper (dissertation director), Jack Jobst, Dennis Lynch, Dave Poplowski (from Computer Science at MTU), and Pat Sullivan (outside reader from Purdue University).

Second, I thank the legion of volunteer and partially paid undergraduate and graduate consultants who have contributed to the constant redesign of the Center for Computer-Assisted Language Instruction (CCLI) over the last several decades. I have been consistently impressed, even awed, by their willingness to research, learn, teach, share, negotiate, and give their time in service to this community. What I know about community and sustainability, I have learned from them over the years. My greatest professional pleasure (and trauma) is to watch them graduate and hear about their lives and families postgraduation.

But the most significant influence on this book and my life—as anyone who knows us will testify—has been the unwavering support, endless energy, and simple love of Cindy Selfe. After 30 years, still my soul mate and role model. I give thanks to her and all my friends in Houghton, America for keeping things weird enough to survive in this odd academic world.

1

THE RELATED CHALLENGES OF DIGITAL LITERACY AND THE DYNANIC OF BLAME

SUMMARY OF TOPICS

▶ The Link Between Literacy and Computers Is Forged (p. 2)
▶ The Role of English and Language Arts Teachers (p. 7)
▶ The Dynamic of Blame (p. 8)
▶ People, First; Pedagogy, Second; and Technology, Third (p. 12)
▶ Some Challenges to This Planning Process (p. 13)

This chapter outlines two important and related challenges that computer-using teachers of English and language arts face within their programs, departments, schools, and institutions. First, it describes the increasingly close relationship between literacy and computer technology that characterizes our culture and the complex set of responsibilities that this emerging relationship places on English and language arts teachers. Second, it details some of the pragmatic strains that result as teachers, staff, and administrators attempt to adjust to changing literacy patterns in classrooms, labs, online learning, and teaching environments. Those strains result in a debilitating dynamic of blame that negatively affects the teaching and learning environments of programs and departments that encourage the use of computer technology.

Finally, as a way to address these two related challenges, this chapter provides a general formula that can help teachers and curriculum designers retain a more stable perspective on the technological issues they face: people, first; pedagogy, second; technologies, third. Although this formula is not meant to provide a rigid prescriptive approach to all technology questions, it can help teachers keep their priorities straight as they navigate within the increasingly complex technological landscape of American literacy education.

THE LINK BETWEEN LITERACY AND COMPUTERS IS FORGED

"Literacy, alone, is no longer our business," Cynthia Selfe wrote in 1999:

> the real work facing teachers involves transforming our current limited discussions about technological literacy into more fully informed debates acknowledging the complex relationship between technology, literacy, education, power, economic conditions, and political goals. It is only after we have undertaken this work that we can make any productive change. (pp. xxi–xxii)

As Selfe went on to explain, by the end of the 20th century, literacy instruction for teachers of English and language arts had become fundamentally and inextricably linked with computer-based systems of digital communication. Further this relationship had come to have a direct bearing on the work that literacy specialists undertook every day. By the end of the 20th century computer technology had become part of the responsibility as literacy educators—regardless of whether teachers recognized it, or wanted it to be so.

A brief historical examination can provide some perspective on the way in which this link between computers and literacy has been forged over the last two decades. The first fully assembled microcomputers began appearing in English and language arts classrooms in the early 1980s. At this time, the enthusiasm for these machines ran high. One of the major hopes for computers was that they could somehow help democratize American classrooms. As the culturally informed reasoning went in the early 1980s, if the nation could put enough computers into enough schools, then all students—regardless of socioeconomic status (SES), race, or gender—would have access to technology and, thus, to success in a culture that was sure to be increasingly dependent on technology.

By 1994, 68.4% of 4th-grade students, 82.3% of 8th-grade students, and 86.9% of 11th-grade students were writing stories or papers on computers (*The Condition of Education 1997*, 1997). At the same time, 43% of 4th-grade teachers and 17% of 8th-grade teachers reported using computers to teach reading (Coley, Crandler, & Engle, 1997). By 1996, Dr. Kenneth Green reported that

> In virtually all sectors of the economy, schools, colleges, homes, and the workplace, computers and information technology have made the transition from the unique to the ubiquitous. Consequently, colleges confront growing expectations from students across all disciplines that technology will be part of the learning and instructional experience.

> (http://ericir_syr.edu/Projects/Campus_computing/1996.index.html)

By 1997, only 3 years later, 98% of all schools owned at least some computers, and the ratio of computers to students, at 1 to 10, was at an all-time low (Coley, Crandler, & Engler, 1997). By 2004, it had become increasingly difficult to find English studies programs at the collegiate level or language arts program at the elementary and secondary level that had *not* invested heavily in computer-based instruction and that has not used computers to teach literacy. Most schools by this time had recognized an obligation to educate citizens to communicate effectively within electronic environments.

In part the linkage between literacy and technology developed so rapidly because it was congruent with Americans' understanding of the increasingly technological world in which citizens were functioning and with their belief in the power of education. The goal of integrating technology into school curricula was to provide students a set of marketable skills that outfitted them for employment after graduation from high school or college, and to produce a technologically skilled citizenry that could contribute to the national commonwealth.

This same goal directly informed the ways in which literacy and technology were codified in federal legislation on education, state performance frameworks, and the standards documents of various professional organizations. In 1994, for instance, the Goals 2000: Educate America Act, which aimed to "raise expectations for students by setting challenging academic standards," included the following language in Section 231. It illustrates just how many approaches the national government would take to infuse computing technologies into our educational systems:

It is the purpose of this part to promote achievement of the National Education Goals and—

(1) to provide leadership at the Federal level, through the Department of Education, by developing a national vision and strategy—

    (A) to infuse technology and technology planning into all educational programs and training functions carried out within school systems at the State and local level;

    (B) to coordinate educational technology activities among the related Federal and State departments or agencies, industry organizations;

    (C) to establish working guidelines to ensure maximum interoperability nationwide and ease of access for the emerging technologies so that no school system will be excluded from the technological revolution; and

    (D) to ensure that Federal technology-related policies and programs facilitate the use of technology in education;

(2) to promote awareness of the potential of technology for improving teaching and learning;

(3) to support State and local efforts to increase the effective use of technology for education;

(4) to demonstrate ways in which technology can be used to improve teaching and learning, and to help ensure that all students have an equal opportunity to meet State education standards;

(5) to ensure the availability and dissemination of knowledge (drawn from research and experience) that can form the basis for sound State and local decisions about investment in, and effective uses of, educational technology;

(6) to promote high-quality professional development opportunities for teachers and administrators regarding the integration of technology into instruction and administration;

(7) to promote the effective uses of technology in existing Federal education programs, such as chapter 1 of title I of the Elementary and Secondary Education Act of 1965 and vocational education programs; and

(8) to monitor, advancements in technology to encourage the development of effective educational uses of technology. ("HR 1804, Goals 2000: Educate America Act," 1994, Section 213)

In response to the goals identified by the federal government, state education departments and professional societies also began to identify and adopt a range of content-area standards documents.

By 1995, for example, the state of Michigan—in the Michigan Curriculum Framework: Content Standards & Benchmarks—included the following "Vision Statement" for teachers of English Language Arts, describing a "literate individual," in part, as one who

> communicates skillfully and effectively through printed, visual, auditory, and technological media in the home, school, community, and workplace. (p. 3)

Under the "Inquiry and Research" content standard, this document continued,

> [Students will] explain and use resources that are most appropriate and readily available for investigating a particular question or topic. Examples include knowledgeable people, field trips, tables of contents, indexes, glossaries, icons/headings, hypertext, storage addresses, CD-ROM/laser disks, electronic mail, and library catalogue databases. (p. 20)

Similarly, by 1996, the National Council of Teachers of English (NCTE) and the International Reading Association (IRA) had published the first *Standards for English Language Arts* document in the history of that organization. Within this document, 12 standards were identified. Of these, Standard #8 read,

> Students use a variety of technological and informational resources (e.g., libraries, databases, computer networks, video) to gather and synthesize information and to create and communicate knowledge. (p. 39)

The language in the NCTE/IRA (1996) standard provided a snapshot of the commonsense assumptions about technology and its links to literacy that Americans held at that time:

> To take advantage of the resources that technology offers and to become prepared for the demands that will face them in the future, students need to learn how to use an array of technologies, from computers and computer networks to electronic mail, interactive video, and CD-ROMs. Technology opens up new worlds to students, making

available a tremendous assortment of information, ideas, and images. It also provides new motivation for writing and allows students to assume greater responsibility for their own learning. . . .

Students should use computers, then, to compose texts and graphics for themselves and others and to publish their own works. This requires skill in keyboarding and word processing as students draft, revise, and edit their writing, seeking feedback from peers and teachers along the way. Students should use computers individually and collaboratively to develop and publish a variety of works. . . . Also, extended use of computers should be encouraged when connection to a network makes it possible to correspond with others nearby or far away. (pp. 39–40)

By the end of the end of the 20th century, then, the national definition of literacy had become inextricably intertwined with computer technology in American schools. As a report issued by Secretary of Education Richard Riley noted,

[Technological literacy involves] computer skills and the ability to use computers and other technology to improve learning, productivity, and performance. (*Getting America's Students Ready for the 21st Century*, 1996, p. 5)

This definition of *technological literacy*—and what has been called *digital literacy*—alluded not only to people's functional understanding of what computers are and how they are used, or their basic familiarity with the mechanical skills of keyboarding, storing information, and retrieving it. Rather, it suggested a new set of terms—*technological literacy* or *digital literacy*—to refer to a complex set of socioculturally situated values, practices, and skills involved in operating linguistically within the context of electronic environments—including reading, writing, and composing in many different media. The term *technological literacy* (and the variant I used here, *digital literacy*) was meant to link computing technologies and literacy at fundamental levels of both conception and social practice. In this context, digital literacy referred to sociocultural contexts for discourse and communication, as well as the social and linguistic products and practices of communication, and the ways in which electronic communication environments had become essential parts of our cultural understanding of, and valuing of, what it meant to be literate. The unfortunate result of using this sort of short hand (i.e., digital literacy) is that it can work to mask what should be obvious here: that such literacy practices are quite complex, always changing, and much more than the skills lists we often see associated with computer literacy. I can only hope that the reader keeps in mind the inherent complexity implied by *digital literacy* as we unpack and further complicate the infrastructures behind this term.

THE ROLE OF ENGLISH AND LANGUAGE ARTS TEACHERS

Despite the increasingly close relationship between literacy and digital technology, however, not all English and language arts teachers have been able to identify an active role for themselves in managing technology or shaping computer-supported teaching and learning environments.

At one level, this situation exists because many English and language arts teachers lack the professional development they need to be confident participants in setting technology policy and shaping technology practices. In 1996, for instance:

- Only 14% of public school teachers had more than 8 hours of training (in-service or professional development programs) in the area of educational technology in the 1993-94 school year.
- As many as 50% of teachers have little or no experience at all with technology in the classroom.
- Much current professional development is in the form of one-shot seminars that are insufficient to bring the teaching profession up to speed with emerging technologies.
- Currently, only 18 states require training in technology for all teachers seeking certification, and only 5 require technology training for teacher in-service. (*Getting America's Students Ready for the 21st Century*, 1996, p. 280)

At another level, this situation holds true because many English studies, composition, and language arts teachers are most comfortable maintaining the culture's conventional separation of the arts and technology (cf. Snow, 1964; Latour, "Preface," *Aramis*, 1996) as it has historically structured the responsibilities of English studies professionals. This historical separation has allowed teachers of English and language arts to use computer technology in their homes, offices, and classrooms while generally absolving them from the responsibility for planning for technology; thinking critically about technology; systematically assessing the value of technology; or making the difficult decisions associated with technological infrastructures and policies in their programs, schools, and institutions (cf. Hawisher & Selfe, 1998; R. Selfe, 1998; Selfe & Selfe, 1994).

Whatever its cause, English and language arts teachers' lack of professional involvement in setting technology policy and managing technology practices at the local level has become increasingly problematic. It is related, among other effects, to situations in which

- states are allowed to mandate standards for technological literacy without providing guidance about how to manage technological change in schools or the resources needed to support teachers,
- administrators are allowed to set technology policies that have a negative impact on teachers' abilities to use technology effectively in their own classrooms,
- teachers are required to use computers in their classrooms without having been afforded adequate access to the professional development they need to do so effectively, and
- schools and institutions dependent on technological systems that are designed to meet the goals of technicians or administrators rather than those of teachers and students.

Collectively, and in concert with the rapid pace of technological change in general, these effects can serve to reinforce English and language arts teachers' perceptions that they are powerless to shape computer-supported teaching and learning environments—even at the local level of programs, departments, and schools. Such effects can also contribute to a debilitating dynamic of blame that distracts teachers, administrators, and staff members from being active, critical, and productive managers of technology in their classrooms, schools, and institutions.

THE DYNAMIC OF BLAME

What is the dynamic of blame? How does it function within programs, schools, and departments? What are its effect on teachers of English and language arts? Although the specific configurations of this dynamic vary at each institution, the general phenomenon depends on the perception that technological changes, policies, and practices are controlled by others who make decisions contrary to one's own needs. In response to this feeling—and in the absence of accurate information about the constraints under which other people are operating—individuals become convinced that they are powerless to shape teaching and learning environments effectively.

Most often the dynamic of blame begins with individuals, often teachers, who feel their efforts to integrate computers into a curriculum enjoy less support than they deserve and require. Consider, for instance, the comments of Mary M., a teacher committed to establishing and sustaining an effective computer-supported teaching efforts within her department:

> Money and adequate facilities as well as campus wide support are problems. They want us to do it [teach using communication technologies], just do it without costing any money or having campus wide planning of technology and funding.

> Information [T]echnology [the administrative department or unit] which is responsible for the other labs on campus will not give technical support to the writing center nor to the teaching of English with computer enhancement. It is difficult to schedule or use lab facilities to even provide minimal training to whole classes of students in the use of technology on the net or on the campus network. Territories are defined, and it seems that [I]nformation [T]echnology [the IT unit] does not want to be a part of providing services to students who are in specific classes, but only to operate labs, give scheduled training classes that cannot possibly reach all students, and let anyone else hang.

Teachers like Mary, who are enthusiastic supporters of technology, but feel powerless to obtain the kinds of resources needed to increase computer support for their classes, participate in the dynamic by blaming program or school administrators (not entirely unjustly) for failing to provide adequate financing. In response, administrators who must justify departmental expenditures to school boards, but feel inadequate to the task of setting productive departmental priorities about technology, often resort to blaming these innovative teachers for making so many costly demands on already strained departmental budgets. Figure 1.1 is a representation of a dynamic of blame, which I describe in more detail in the following paragraphs.

Nor are teachers and administrators the only individuals who may become involved in this dynamic of blame—other stakeholders in digital literacy systems, such as staff members, colleagues who do not use com-

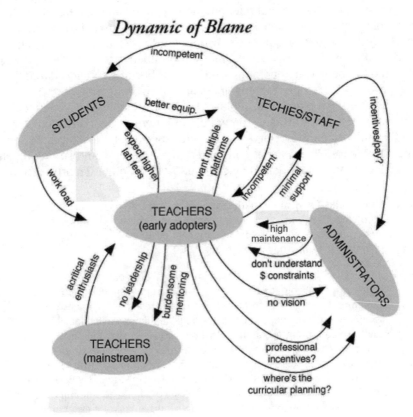

Figure 1.1 A Dynamic of Blame.

puters, and students, are also involved. For example, the same English and language arts teachers who want to offer more ambitious computer-supported, courses—but do not have the background to configure computer systems to support their efforts, often blame technical support staff for failing to undertake their own projects in a timely manner. Technology staff members—overworked on many fronts—may, in turn, blame those teachers who demand scarce computer resources for courses that have gotten along for years with no computer support at all.

Nor does the dynamic necessarily stop there. It may be exacerbated by other teachers of English and language arts who are less enthusiastic about computer-supported classes and less confident about their abilities to teach such courses. These teachers may contribute to the dynamic by blaming computer-using teachers for raising the expectations of students who then demand more technology in all their classes or for spending departmental monies on computers rather than on the books needed to supplement inadequate library resources. The teachers who are enthusiastic about using computers may, in turn, blame their more reluctant colleagues for blocking new technology projects that might benefit students or for voting against proposals to update departmental computer holdings. In a similar vein, students who consider their future tied to their ability to communicate in technological environments may criticize teachers who refuse to teach their classes in computer-supported environments. Teachers who hesitate to undertake the integration of technology without adequate opportunities for professional development may blame students for mindlessly demanding the most sophisticated and eye-catching computers without regard to the appropriateness of such systems.

Other individuals who have a stake in technological literacy decisions may also participate in the dynamic of blame: Parents and employers often blame schools and teachers for doing an inadequate job of preparing students for an increasingly technological world, but at the same time complain about the increasing cost of higher education or constant millage proposals driven by technology upgrades. Software and hardware vendors blame teachers for failing to take advantage of new educational products, and legislators blame schools and teachers for a lack of initiative in integrating technology into classrooms.

By the time a dynamic of blame is fully established, it may look like the diagram in Fig. 1. Unfortunately, such a dynamic is founded on some very real problems—each stakeholder identified in this diagram has his or her own *appropriate* concerns about technology, and each is also constrained by his or her own individual ability to shape technology policies and practices. It is easy to imagine how much energy—largely unproductive in nature—might be expended in this dynamic. This is primarily because each stakeholder has only a limited understanding of the pressures and social contexts that frame the lives of others working in and around technology-rich environments.

Such a dynamic can result in paralysis, misdirection, and a lack of productive action. It can also mask the more productive ways in which teams of stakeholders can act collectively to leverage pedagogical and institution al change that support appropriate and critical approaches to technology-rich learning environments.

Because so many teachers of English and language arts are confronted with overdetermined environments that support rapid technological change—and because they often lack the support that effective and ongoing programs of professional development can provide—it is hard to see how one might *not* become drawn into a dynamic of blame. Without alternative strategies for coping with such technological challenges, this dynamic may offer these teachers the only way to deal with the challenges technology has presented them.

PEOPLE, FIRST; PEDAGOGY, SECOND; AND TECHNOLOGY, THIRD

So how can literacy professionals deal more productively with overdetermined technological change and the considerable pressures generated by the literacy–computer linkage in America's schools? In this book, I suggest a series of strategies based on the following set of priorities: people, first; pedagogy, second; and technology, third.

With this sequence of priorities, I do not mean to suggest that teachers can always separate people so neatly from their pedagogical approaches and the technologies they use. Indeed in most programs, there is an intimate interplay between these elements; without all three acting in balance, the success of teaching and learning in technological environments can be seriously compromised.

However, if teachers of English and language arts are to make sense of the complex social and historical articulations that link literacy to computers, if they are to extend the efficacy of their instructional efforts in technological environments, they need to keep their general priorities as humanists straight: focusing first on the literacy needs and talents that students exhibit and the collective talents that teachers, administrators, and staff members can bring to bear on instructional problems. It is only within the context of these human needs and resources that specific pedagogical strategies and approaches for teaching digital literacy will make sense. And it is only when instructional goals lead the way that technological decisions begin to make sense.

Most important, when teachers of English and language arts adopt the People = > Pedagogy = > Technology formulation as an heuristic (not rigidly, as a rule), they also construct themselves into an active role in relation to technology decisions. In such a relationship, teachers participate in technology decision making—basing their own input on the foundation of their background as humanists and literacy specialists, rather than simply on their needs as technology users. This sense of agency is important if teachers are to take on the expanded agenda laid out in the Preface of this book, building technology-rich educational environments that focus on the needs of students and the teaching of literacy, English and language arts, and—perhaps most important—creating a culture of support that can sustain and nurture such environments.

SOME CHALLENGES TO
THIS PLANNING PROCESS

This heuristic or planning process has had its critics. Good colleagues have had reasonable concerns about a process that emphasizes people first, pedagogy second, and technologies third. The critique has come from two camps, which take the following forms:

▶ Some claim that it's impossible (and unproductive) to find an entire faculty (much less a faculty, a student body, the staff, and immediate administrators as I suggest in chap. 2) willing to agree on the exact wording and content of a set of goals for teaching or teaching with communication technologies (Kemp, 2000). Why then insist on setting collective goals before launching new technology-rich instructional projects? The effort to come to consensus will simply make your digital design or redesign improbable if not impossible.

▶ Others claim (quite reasonably) that the technologies often lead to changes in our goals and working environments because they afford us educational opportunities that never existed before (Reiss, personal correspondence). If we attend primarily to people and pedagogy, won't we miss opportunities to take advantage of new technologies? Why not make the most innovative communication technologies the focus of our attention?

In answer, let me begin with a brief institutional history that seems important and revealing. The MTU commitment to this process began even before Cindy Selfe instituted the Computers in Writing Intensive Classes (CIWIC[1]) summer workshops about 17 years ago. Yet the process is re-

---

[1]To see the most recent versions of this suit of workshops, go to http://www.hu. mtu.edu/ciwic.

established and reinvigorated each year in that workshop, so I'll use it as the basis for my argument. Seventeen years ago, we started by asking participants to consider their core teaching values: What human literacy needs were we trying to address in our classes? These values eventually became the instructional and operational goals that helped drive the use and design of technology-rich environments that participants hoped to run, use, develop, or influence. The process that teachers work through during the first day and half of a 2-week workshop (see the Subsection A Planning Process in chap. 3) is essentially the same today as it was in 1989, when Cindy Selfe wrote the following in *Creating a Computer-Supported Writing Facility: A Blueprint for Action.*

> To build a successful computer-supported writing center, to sustain operations, and eventually to improve the support such a facility provides, English composition teachers need to start with what hey know about writing and teaching rather than what they know about technology (p. xxi)

Of course English and language arts teachers no longer talk simply about writing in these spaces, but recognize the need to have students communicate or compose in many media. We no longer talk simply about labs, centers, and computer-supported classrooms when there are online environments to consider. Yet the process that Selfe sketched out in the first three chapters of that book has remained remarkably stable and is intended to encourage interested English studies and language arts stakeholders to design environments that grow directly out of the context of an existing communication program: an environment that is shaped by established communication-intensive courses and informed by the shared pedagogical values of a particular faculty and staff.

In the early 1980s, when CIWIC began, it seemed feasible and desirable to convince a departmental faculty to sign on to one particular vision for teaching composition. The Humanities department of Michigan Technological University (MTU) had just completed over a decade of writing-across-the-curriculum workshops where Carol Berkenkotter, Beth Flynn, Randy Freisinger, Toby Fulwiler, Diana George, Bruce Petersen, Cindy Selfe, Billie Wahlstom, Art Young, and others had made a case for writing instruction across the disciplines at a largely engineering-oriented university. That effort shaped our department's common understanding of communication instruction in ways that other departments at other institutions might not have experienced.

This history suggests, in partial answer to the questions of Fred Kemp, that other institutions might look for and already have had the same type of formative experience as a result of communication initiatives with names like writing across the curriculum, communication across the curriculum, and electronic communication across the curriculum (cf. Reiss, Selfe, and Young). Others have gone or might yet go through the same type of process as they work to establish and maintain online and onsite writing, communication, and learning centers. Initiatives of this type (including some efforts to develop ubiquitous computing programs and online or distance learning programs) have helped and will help shape commonly held approaches to language arts and communication instruction. For those institutions, our original suggestion—that before you go further with technology initiatives, you try to arrive at some type of relative consensus about communication goals—will make sense.

Yet even at institutions without these formative experiences, the value of discussing and refining instructional and operational goals before making the social, technological, and architectural decisions that surround technology-rich environments is a valuable exercise. At our 2-week workshop, CIWIC, these days teachers are asked to imagine goals on which a *substantial corps* of technology leaders can agree. Coming to a consensus over such goals for an entire faculty may be overly optimistic, but going it alone, although tempting, often leads to short-lived initiatives that are unsustainable (as I claim in chap. 2). What we do state at the outset is that we recognize that literacy professionals already have a strong dialectical relationship to technology. That is, what they perceive as instructional needs and eventually develop as operational goals are highly dependent on their previous experiences with technology and their internal vision of what digital technologies can do for them and their students. Indeed I recognize that human needs never really precede technologies: They are "mutually constructing systems" (J. Johnson-Eilola, personal correspondence, April 17, 2003); the needs and technologies reconstruct each other in an interesting and dynamic way. As a heuristic, however, the People = > Pedagogy = > Technology formulation works well for political and historical reasons. Consider the following.

The history of the discipline in the mid-1980s also influenced the way those at MTU approached the technologies. In those earlier years, we heard little *besides* discussions of this or that technology: what I refer to as "bits and bytes" discussions. In response, we sought to initiate dialogues that focused on the human and pedagogical components of our projects, the human side of these cyborg systems. It is possible that we may not have given the technical components of promising environments the credit they deserve for creating educational change.[2] Yet we still insist that an emphasis on human goals and objectives is a valuable first exercise before one begins speculating on the value or changes occurring because of specific technologies. We have clung to this process for several reasons:

▶ Theprocess forces us to attend to students', teachers', and institutional needs.

▶ The process makes the pedagogical assumptions of key stakeholders and developers of a project explicit and thus operational.

▶ The process provides academics interested in communication-based pedagogy with a position of strength from which to argue when they describe their digital intentions to technology experts, strapped administrators, or skeptical colleagues.

Most readers will also recognize that the bits and bytes discussions are still with us. Technical people want to talk primarily about the technology, and it is something we have to struggle to overcome. It works two ways. After several decades of practice, I have found that one of the fastest ways to get technicians to glaze over is to begin talking about instructional goals. We can also watch our literacy colleagues glaze over once we start to talk about technology. This must change, and those of us who honestly believe in the computer–literacy linkage must help each group understand the exciting possibilities that the other offers.

As a result of these productive criticisms, we have modified our process to some extent without changing it entirely. For instance, we do not expect every group of innovators, an entire program, or an institution to come to a consensus over goals and objectives before beginning technology-rich projects. Yet we still propose that such discussions must be at the heart of the ongoing design of technology-rich environments in English studies and language arts programs. We do and always have focused at some point in the design process on the technologies themselves. For instance, we see online environments running off of Web-based database systems as increasingly important to English studies and language arts professionals and try to point people toward colleagues and commercial ven-

---

[2]Though some theorists do agree that we should be cautious about attributing cultural or educational change to new computing technologies: Landauer's *The Trouble with Computers.*

dors who are developing such systems. Most course-management systems like WebCT, BlackBoard, and NiceNet (a free service as of September 2002) as well as search engines are based around online databases; educational MOOs[3] sited around the country rely on backend databases. Fred Kemp's TOPICs environment at Texas Tech < http://english.ttu.edu:5555 > and Peg Syverson's Learning Records Online at the University of Texas < http://lro.cwrl.utexas.edu > are both taking advantage of these technologies.[4] XML projects that deliver the same content in many different forms (print, Web, and PDF) are increasingly used in libraries and available to academics interested in teaching with technology.

All of the most useful systems or technologies available to English studies and language arts professionals, however, are successful because they offer pedagogical opportunities and fill institutional needs, not simply because they are cutting edge. This planning process, then, encourages literacy professionals to make choices based on pedagogical assumptions and institutional needs—which those professionals understand quite well—and not simply technological efficacy. Quite frequently and unfortunately, teachers find themselves facing the latter rather than the former.

The following are sustainable practices that illustrate how high school and college literacy educators have attended to people, pedagogy, and technology in the design and creation of alternative, productive, technology-rich centers.

---

[3]MOO's are online environments (virtual spaces) that allow for programming, the building and describing of objects like rooms, robots (bots), and media projects (texts and others). They are spaces often used to chat in real time. In short they are more robust versions of the ubiquitous instant messaging systems we see many young people using these days.

[4]Please read the well-developed explanation of these systems at the web sites provided.

One interesting trend at the collegiate level is the development of learning centers that recognize the need for technology-rich literacy support for courses across the curriculum. Indeed these centers, which often support the work of both students and teachers (and in this case, parents as well!), are influenced by several long-established movements in English studies and language arts programs across the country: writing centers, which are focused on small-group and one-to-one peer instruction and support; collaborative learning projects; communication-across-the-curriculum programs; and the integrated use of technology-rich facilities and online environments in support of teaching. These have been combined at times in centers like Pam Childer's < pchilder@ mccallie.org > Caldwell Writing Center at The McCallie School in Chattanooga, Tennessee and Furman University's CCLC, created and designed under the direction of James Inman, now at the University of Southern Florida < jinman@english.cas.usf.edu > . (Dickie Selfe)

The Caldwell Writing Center at The McCallie School in Chattanooga, Tennessee

Pam Childers, The McCallie School

Many secondary school writing centers focus on writing across the curriculum with technology as a major component of the program. Supporting both students and faculty through interdisciplinary projects involving critical thinking skills and improved writing, the writing center uses technology as part of individual, collaborative, and group support. Integrated use of technology through online Web sites, Internet research and writing, and e-mail communication provide unique teaching and learning opportunities for both students and faculty. The Caldwell Writing Center at The McCallie School in Chattanooga, Tennessee, has been operating since 1991 and continues to experiment with ways to integrate technology into the teaching and learning of students and staff.

Changing our Focus

Pam Childers writes,

I have managed to sustain the writing center by changing focus, interacting with students, faculty, and administration in new and different ways.

At first it was more of a student-focused, face-to-face facility with faculty coming in for assistance with class and maybe a few writing assignments. Computers started as tools for improving writing or for faculty to easily write and store assignments. We had a LAN (local area network) so teachers could have students drop work into their folders. With the introduction of e-mail, the Internet accessibility, faculty and students learned new ways to interact with the writing center. Our Web site <http://www.mccallie.org/wrt_ctr> has become important for research and professional resources. I started with some student "tutors" or assistants who volunteered, then we added a peer tutoring course that only had a few independent study students each year. In 2 years, I added a part-time assistant, which enabled me to get into the classroom more to work with students and faculty, and to attend meetings that were important for WAC and writing instruction. We also now do more online responses to the writing of students and faculty through e-mail attachments. The administrative relationship has mainly changed because the cast of characters has changed. I am now trusted more with responsibilities; my opinions are considered in planning, and I think they may actually know what I do!

The funding for the CWC has also changed over the years. The budget has decreased because money has been allocated in different accounts: Technology now comes from Technology Department budget, and an assistant salary comes from a separate account. As a result, the CWC has become institutionalized. I have managed to obtain funds for anything I really need. The most important part of the effort is in producing annual reports and letters to those who have endowed the chair I hold to make them happy and keep the money flowing! I guess the bottom line is to make a WAC-based writing center a necessity rather than a luxury. If people assume it is there and assume that it must have an annual budget, then it will. Public relations and student, faculty and parental support help make that all possible.

For more information, contact Pamela B. Childers, Ed.D., Caldwell Chair of Composition (423-493-5849) or visit<http://www.mccallie. org/wrt_ctr> and <http://www.mccallie.org/science/mlowry/Oceans ClassFolder/Oceansweb.html>.

Center for Collaborative Learning and Communication (CCLC), Furman University

James Inman, University of South Florida

In October 2000, Furman University's Center for Collaborative Learning and Communication (CCLC) first opened its doors, marking the end of more than 3 years of advance planning by an interdisciplinary team of faculty, staff, students, and administrators.

CCLC's ambitious mission is "To promote and support writing, communication, and technology excellence and to facilitate and encourage collaborative teaching and learning at Furman University among faculty, staff, and students." To accomplish this mission, CCLC takes writing center pedagogy's emphasis on one-to-one peer conversation and writer empowerment and expands it to include not only writing, but also speaking and technology. CCLC reaches out to all members of the Furman community, including faculty, staff, and students, as well as their families.

CCLC's design emphasizes multiple modes of learning, seeking to support the broadest possible range of teaching and learning styles. Core areas include the following:

- Informal Gathering Areas: Small spaces with comfy chairs for group conversation and planning and with multiple laptop plugs;
- Collaborative Workstations: Areas designed for project development that feature an L-shaped table with a single computer and a round table with four chairs for collaboration;
- Computer Consultation Stations: Private spaces with a single computer and two chairs designed for learning technology; and
- Multimedia Studios: Rooms dedicated to multimedia production and editing, as well as oral presentation rehearsal.

We invite CCLC visitors to reinvent these areas by moving furniture around and to suggest additions or changes to the Center at large, hoping this emphasis on versatility and conversation will help CCLC's mission to be sustained over time.

Because of its large-scale mission and the current emphasis on technology in both writing and communication practice, CCLC maintains an impressive suite of computers and multimedia technologies:

- Fifteen PC platform machines featuring an array of hardware, including a flatbed scanner, a photo and slide scanner, QuickCams, a digital video camera, and a projector, as well as internal CD-writers and two 21" monitors;

- Three Macintosh platform machines, including a flatbed scanner and an external CD-writer;

- Three printers, one black-and-white for high-volume laser printing, one color for staff use, and one small black-and-white for staff laser printing; and

- A variety of publishing and communications software, including Microsoft *Office*, Netscape *Communicator*, *Internet Explorer*, Adobe *Photoshop* and *Pagemaker*, and Macromedia *Dreamweaver* and *Fireworks*, as well as the Furman standard mailer *Lotus Notes*.

We also plan regular assessments of the Furman community's technology needs, with our plan being to provide updates as appropriate to ensure CCLC's environment is sustainable as a campus technology leader.

CCLC's core team includes a tenure-line director, an administrative secretary, eight student peer consultants, and an advisory committee of faculty, students, and staff. The director's position, previously held by computers and writing scholar James A. Inman, proved to be especially innovative. It is tenure line, but tenure is not associated with a particular department, instead given generally under the arm of academic affairs. The tenured members of the CCLC advisory committee make up the tenure and promotion committee.

Also innovative is the training program for CCLC peer consultants. They must complete a semester-long course, and the latest version, entitled "Teaching One-to-One in Real and Virtual Environments," has recently won approval as a permanent catalog course at Furman. Students explore planning, practice, assessment, and research activities associated with pedagogy. The most significant innovation is that all consultants must be proficient in each core area of CCLC: writing, communication, and technology. The logic for placing such broad responsibility on consultants is that they will develop a savvy means of learning new aspects of practice, which will ensure that their learning is sustained into the future.

2

ESTABLISHING A CULTURE OF SUPPORT WITHIN WHICH TEACHERS COME FIRST, PEDAGOGY SECOND, AND TECHNOLOGY THIRD

SUMMARY OF TOPICS

▶ Moving From a Dynamic of Blame to a Culture of Support: Three Steps (p. 24)
- Recognizing the Need for Support (p. 24)
- Involving Teachers (p. 26)
- Identifying Primary Stakeholders (p. 28)
▶ Characteristics of Successful Cultures of Support (p. 41)

This chapter introduces a productive alternative to the dynamic of blame described in chap. 1. *Culture of support* is the term I use to describe this alternative approach—I mean it to refer to an ensemble, team-driven effort that can help sustain the teaching of literacy in innovative, technology-rich environments.

The chapter begins by describing three initial steps that an English or language arts program can take to develop a locally viable culture of support. The first step seems, on its face, to be quite obvious: A department, program, or entire school district must begin by recognizing the kinds of support that teachers require to integrate technology—in meaningful ways—into English and language arts classes and then commit itself to creating a culture that supports this effort. The actual implementation of this step, however, is quite complex and highly dependent on local pedagogical, fiscal, and institutional conditions. The second step describes how and why teachers of English and language arts can and should assume a leadership role in creating and sustaining such a culture of support. The third step involves identifying a range of primary or interested stakeholders who see the benefits of establishing and participating in such an effort.

MOVING AWAY FROM THE DYNAMIC OF BLAME AND TOWARD A CULTURE OF SUPPORT

Without foresight and planning for technology use, many departments of English and language arts respond to national, state, district, or institutional technology initiatives by undertaking short-term strategies that answer immediate problems—creating a new computer-supported writing facility with an unexpected grant of money, encouraging teachers to integrate technology into their classes using their own time and resources, or purchasing a software package that claims to address students' most pressing writing and language problems. In contrast, departments, programs, and districts need to plan for long-term sustainable efforts that will support teachers of English and language arts on an ongoing basis by taking up the difficult task of changing the way departments think about teaching literacy with technology.

Step 1: Recognizing the Support Required to Integrate Technology in Meaningful Ways in English Studies and Language Arts Classes

The first step in moving away from a dynamic of blame and toward a culture of support requires that a department recognize the challenges involved in teaching literacy studies within technological environments. When English and language arts teachers describe the challenges of integrating technology into their classes and lessons, they most often point to the following factors:

- a lack of time to prepare lessons, learn new technologies, and experiment;
- a lack of technical support when they are trying to learn new technologies, teach in technological environments, discover how technologies can improve their teaching, and make technology do what they want it to do;
- a lack of systematic, professionally relevant training by other computer-using English and language arts teachers who can

show them the best practices and suggest strategies for supporting these practices in local school and technological environments;

- the lack of convenient access to technology, in their classrooms,
offices, and homes where they can plan and experiment with
technology;
- the lack of opportunity to participate in meaningful ways in
shaping technology policy and making technology decisions
that will affect their own teaching and the learning of students
in their classrooms (e.g., deciding how computer-supported
teaching efforts are evaluated in tenure and promotion guidelines, collaborating with other teachers on the scheduling guidelines for assigned lab times, determining how classroom technologies and computer-supported classrooms and labs are funded within an institution; deciding who owns the copyright to
online instructional materials that teachers and students create).

These challenges, however, need not be paralyzing. In fact they can
provide a specific starting place for departments and programs committed
to avoiding when possible a debilitating dynamic of blame. Working from
these specific needs, computer-using teachers of English and language arts
can begin the process of creating a culture of support that realistically
addresses the challenges generated by literacy education in a technological
age. In particular, such a culture would provide teachers of English and language arts the kind of help they need to:

- learn new technologies,
- plan and integrate these technologies into their classes and lessons,
- implement technological innovations in technology-rich facilities or online environments,
- assess the effectiveness of teaching and learning that occurs,
and
- plan for the next experimental iteration of technology-rich lessons and classes.

Although the concept of creating a culture of support seems simple
enough, the actual effort of providing such an environment generally
proves quite complex, politicized, and often expensive. At the same time,
however, most institutions recognize the importance of educating students
to communicate effectively within technological environments and, given
this recognition, are willing to provide teachers some level of technical and

institutional support to encourage such efforts—especially if teachers are willing to participate more actively in integrating technology into their classes and managing technology in responsible ways. The bottom line is that teachers should be able to *expect* some level of support for their work in integrating technology into their classes. At the same time, however, they should also *expect* to assume a leadership role in creating an effective culture of support that will sustain their efforts.

Step 2: Involving English and Language Arts Teachers in Creating a Culture of Support

Because the cultures of support described in this book focus on the efforts of teaching and learning literacy skills, attitudes, and approaches in technological environments, they necessarily revolve around the efforts and needs of teachers of English and language arts. These teachers must assume a leadership role in creating and maintaining a workable culture of support in their own programs, departments, and districts. After all teachers are the best judges of what help they need to sustain literacy-based, technology-rich teaching practices. In the People = > Pedagogy = > Technology formulation, they are at the source of the needs that eventually drive technology-rich instructional facilities and systems. In addition, they are perhaps the only people who are invested so specifically and directly in such efforts that they are willing to undertake the sustained project of keeping a culture of support going over the long run.

Because of this willingness, invested teachers of English and language arts are some of the best architects of supportive systems—the best individuals to lead the effort to imagine, plan, and implement these cultures in support. One example might help illustrate the value of literacy professionals in the process of integrating communication technologies into the curriculum. From 1999 to the present, MTU has worked with the Delta Schoolcraft Intermediate School District to provide Electronic Communication Across the Curriculum summer workshops for K-12 teacher leaders. Over the years, we might have interacted with 60 teachers (and students who work in their schools), but the district has hundreds of teachers whom they would like to see engage in technology-rich instruction. To help encourage widespread engagement, the DSISD set up their 100% technology training professional development days. On those days, the teachers, only some of whom have attended ECAC summer sessions, organize technology-rich workshops by disciplines and grade levels. They are hands-on and focused on specific classroom practices. For that reason they appeal to those on the front lines of our educational system. DSISD is working on a district-wide culture of support for appropriate integration of technology into the classroom, but they have decided, wisely I think, that such a culture can only be sustained if teaching professionals—those working in the classroom—are engaged in the process.

The 100% participation workshops created by the DSISD is only one manifestation of the leadership role of computer-using teachers of English and language arts. Each department, institution, and district needs to develop their own approach. The following are some appropropriate activities that always seem to occur in and around sustainable technology-rich environments:

- **Constructing innovative, technology-rich teaching activities, units, and curricula.** This is not a book about how to teach with technology, but it is impossible to understate the importance of visionary pedagogical practices. They are often the most persuasive evidence we can offer to justify the fiscal and professional commitments necessary to sustain a culture of support. Appendix 2.1—Techno-pedagogical Explorations: Toward Sustainable Technology-rich Instruction—is an outline of some of the fundamental approaches to teaching with technology that I have used with teachers and graduate students over the years. For a more complete description of these concepts along with specific activities, descriptions of the technologies, as well as warnings that necessarily go along with these activities see, "Techno-pedagogical Explorations: Toward Sustainable Technology-rich Instruction" in Pam Takayoshi and Brian Huot's *Teaching Writing with Computers: An introduction* (2003);
- **Meeting together to identify the goals that should drive computer-supported literacy instruction** within a department or program and the culture of support that will allow them to accomplish such goals;
- **Identifying the complex set of constraints and expectations under which instruction must operate**—social, curricular, fiscal, political, personal, economic, and technical;
- **Educating administrators** on a regular basis about both the benefits of sustaining such a culture and the resources needed to accomplish the job—departmental, institutional, or district wide;
- **Identifying and involving other primary stakeholders**—administrators, technical support staff, students, student workers, teachers, school board members, parents, and so on—in the

effort to maintain a robust sustainable culture of support that addresses the needs of all participants;

- **Creating opportunities for primary stakeholders to meet and talk about the challenges** involved in teaching and learning in technological environments, the constraints under which each group of constituents operates, and the most productive and strategic ways to address these challenges;
- **Implementing projects that shape the culture of support** (e.g., ongoing educational seminars, professional development opportunities, each-one-teach-one open houses, student technology assistant programs). These projects will help teachers accomplish the instructional goals associated with teaching literacy in technological environments;
- **Assessing the program's/department's/school's/district's efforts** to sustain a culture of support and the ability of such a culture to help provide meaningful and innovative literacy instruction in technological environments; and
- **Participating on committees, task forces, and other professional groups that make technology decisions and create technology policy** within a program, department, or institution. Their involvement is crucial to making sure that these decisions and policies support the effective teaching and learning of English and language arts teachers in digital environments.

No one teacher, of course, can sustain such a load. Nor are all these activities of equal importance at every institution. This list is meant to illustrate how important it is to engage not only English and language arts leaders, but also interested and engaged colleagues from the institution or community in our efforts to create cultures of support —whether those colleagues are fellow teachers, administrators, staff, parents, corporate partners, or the students we meet in class.

Step 3: Identifying Primary Stakeholders

As this book indicates, no culture of support can be sustained for long unless it involves a team of individuals who have a stake in effective and innovative literacy instruction in technological environments. Members of such a team often include the following kinds of individuals:

Teacher/leaders—some English and language arts teachers are more willing than others to learn new communication technologies as they emerge and integrate them in meaningful ways into classroom projects and assignments. In Fred Kemp's (Texas Tech University) extensive experience, individual teachers/innovators at all levels are the most important feature in efforts to incorporate technology-rich instruction into our curricula (Kemp, 2000). These leaders, often prone to innovation and taking risks in the classroom, are also confident about their ability to make instruction, generally, and technology, more specifically, work for students. Because they are often breaking new ground with their instruction, technology leaders require a great deal of technical support for their classes. They are also generally willing to share their experiences using technology with other teachers, and they tend to be enthusiastic about the potential of technology. Technology leaders—because they are attracted to new technology applications and believe in their potential—are generally willing to work on behalf of technology use in a program, curriculum, or department: to serve on committees, help administer a computer-supported communication facility or an online service, and offer professional development presentations and demonstrations. If the fit between a department or program and a technology leader is a good one—in terms of a culture of support—they may continue to innovate for a number of years.[1]

---

[1]Luckily, experienced and even resistant individuals who are originally not interested in technology-rich instruction are sometimes convinced or convince themselves of the value of communication systems as those technologies are made available in the department. These people can sometimes be the most valuable advocates for others and may indeed eventually take on a lead role in technology-rich efforts.

John Slatin, a professor at the time and one of three tenured professors who have run the CWRL over these many years (a very unusual circumstance, in my experience), said this of the moment of Kinneavy's comments: "It was a stunning and of course amazingly welcome thing to hear, and it made an enormous impact on me and other members of the faculty, and of course on the grad students in the Lab. I remain grateful to Jim for that, among many other acts and statements that evinced his intellectual adventurousness and generosity and his commitment to excellence in teaching. A great moment" (e-mail correspondence, Nov. 2, 2000). The fact that tenured and revered professors make such statements and that tenured faculty direct the computing efforts for the Rhetoric program at the University of Texas at Austin says a great deal about how important it is to reach out to established, interested, and innovative colleagues.

The lesson then is to keep in touch with the leaders in our academic communities despite the statistics that say that those with experience are less likely to adopt and adapt to new communication technologies. We also need to widen our scope of attention and listen for leadership voices from among other populations in our institutions, the most important of which, from my perspective, are those of the students and student workers all around us.

It is apparently common knowledge that tenured and high-ranking scholars are not often involved in the development of technology-rich pedagogy. This, of course, is not true. Although a high percentage of technology leaders may come from the ranks of young professionals, senior people have made significant contributions to departmental efforts and other technology-rich projects. The following accounts out of the University of Texas, at Austin indicate the importance of senior leadership over time. It has been widely circulated that Dr. Jim Kinneavy, possibly the most widely known classical rhetorician of the post-World War II era, once said after teaching in a computer lab for the first time, "I will never teach in a non-computer classroom again." The following is what Dr. John Slatin, currently a full-professor at the same institution, says about that comment and about the other factors that allowed them to continue their technology-related projects. (*Dickie Selfe*)

Senior Leadership in The Computer Writing and Research Laboratories (CWRL), Division of Rhetoric and Composition, University of Texas, Austin.

John Slatin, The University of Texas at Austin

I've not published the report about Jim Kinneavy's comment, but I was there when he made it and I heard him say it more than once. It was a stunning and of course amazingly welcome thing to say, and it made an enormous impact on me and other members of the faculty, and of course on the grad students in the Lab. I remain grateful to Jim for that, among many other acts and statements that evinced his intellectual adventurousness and generosity and his commitment to excellence in teaching. A great moment.

Or course our most sustained technology-related project at UT Austin is the CWRL itself. Several factors have been critical to the CWRL's sustained success [since 1985]. One of these was and still is the availability of a dedicated physical space where graduate students and others teaching and staffing in the Lab could (and did, and do!) "hang out" whenever their schedules and their interests permit, so that the Lab early became a site for a great deal of informal knowledge-making and knowledge-sharing, for the development of what Etienne

Wenger calls a community of practice characterized by (1) mutual engagement in (2) a joint enterprise, using—and creating!—(3) a shared repertoire of tools, artifacts, ideas, information, etc.

Another factor in this sustained technology project was in getting the English Department, which had administrative oversight of the Lab when I became director in 1989, to agree to give graduate students formal assignments to teach in the Lab; that enabled us to have Lab-based classes officially designated in as "computer assisted" in the University's official course schedule, which in turn meant that we could assess a support fee. Only a third of that fee came back to us, but this was at least the beginnings of a budget and enabled us to buy supplies like cables and diskettes.

Giving the graduate students formal assignments to the Lab meant that they were more free to spend time there, thinking and working and inventing; it also enabled us to work out what was at first an ad hoc arrangement, built out of necessity, whereby grad students spent part of their time teaching in the networked classroom and the remainder of their hours working as support staff. This was critical because it gave the graduate students a vital double perspective on teaching in technologically rich environments: They developed and learned the pedagogical practice at the same time they were learning (and developing) the practices necessary to support pedagogical innovation and effectiveness.

Another factor that I believe to have been vital to the Lab's sustainability was that it has always had a faculty director, someone with disciplinary expertise and a direct interest in the Lab as a site for scholarly as well as pedagogical activity— and someone who had the standing in the English Dept. and, later, the Rhetoric Division, to advocate for the Lab's value to both graduate and undergraduate instruction—someone who could also serve on other faculty committees at department, college, and university levels, thereby becoming involved in the constellations or networks of practice emerging around technology-enhanced teaching and learning and research. That all three directors— Jerome Bump, myself, and now Peg Syverson—have been *tenured* faculty at the time of their taking on the directorship is important, too: All of us have been able to contend, sometimes rather heatedly, with tenured colleagues without fear of jeopardizing our jobs. This is a great personal luxury, but it has been a critical factor in the Lab's survival over the years.

Finally, as a result of the formation of the Division of Rhetoric and Composition, announced in 1992, I was asked to develop a 5-year plan for computing in the Division. That document was an important factor, in that it guided decision making over the years to come—each year we would return to it, assess what we had accomplished, re-evaluate the goals and strategies outlined there, and formulate a new plan for the coming year. That helped us raise a great deal of financial support internally—close to a million dollars. I emphasize this because the money made several things possible: life-cycle financing for equipment so we could stay up to date and provide excellent facilities for all concerned; and salary for a full-time Systems Analyst, who took over administration of the network (thankfully!), rationalized it, developed it, managed it; maintained the equipment in good working order; and helped a great deal in establishing the Lab Web site in late 1993/early 1994, one of the earliest instructionally oriented sites on campus, and now among the largest. Having that position *also* made it possible for us to maintain our own servers rather than outsourcing that task to what is now called Academic Computing. This in turn meant that the Lab community was in a position to continually define and redefine the technological practices and network configurations (including security and permissions) in ways that we believed were commensurate with our pedagogical and scholarly goals—even when the arrangements we had in mind ran counter to the standard practices of computer service organizations.

The importance of these teacher/leaders for recruiting a steady stream of additional leaders does not diminish over time even if a program seems successfully implemented. How, then, do current leaders and administrators find, support, and make effective use of the work of these dedicated people? It is not hard to spot someone who is likely to be an "early adopter" or technology leader. However, these individuals often inhabit positions outside the ranks of the tenured and the tenure-track professionals: positions like those of professional staff (part-time and full-time) instructors, lecturers, adjuncts, substitute teachers, paraprofessionals, writing and learning center staff, community members, parents, graduate students, as well as students and student workers.

These stakeholders are often excluded from particular moments of time and in specific institution contexts when decisions are being made (see chap. 6). These kairotic moments where timing is everything—when decisions are made about budgets, technologies, hiring, access policies, travel funds—are the moments when institutional changes are enacted. Moments like these are points in time when technology leaders should be given a chance to enact what Cindy Selfe calls *small potent gestures*. These gestures, over time, change the directional valence of institutional action (Selfe, 1999). In chapter 5, I suggest that we need to better understand the timing of these moments of intervention and make them accessible to teacher/leaders (and other stakeholders), wherever they reside in the educational environment.

Technology leaders, however, may also demand more than their fair share of departmental resources, technical support, and institutional flexibility. They can prove to be less than understanding of colleagues and students who do not embrace technology or learn technological applications as readily as they do themselves. In addition, early adopters of technologies have usually developed sustainable pedagogies over a number of years.

> They are notorious for telling only the positive aspects of theirs and their students' experiences—mentioning only a few of the motivations involved, a smattering of details about the material conditions under which they work, and a couple of the steps they have taken in order to enact successful technology-rich instructional activities. (Selfe, "Techno-pedagocial," p. 20)

For these reasons and others, technology leaders cannot often sustain a culture of support on their own.

Teacher/users—many English and language arts teachers, given their humanist educational histories, are more cautious in adopting technological approaches to teaching literacy. As a result, they integrate computers into their classes only a piece or an assignment at time. Often these teachers need to see the ways in which technology works well for other colleagues before they try different applications and projects. Sometimes they need to be convinced that computers will help them teach a better class than they could without computers.

Teachers who want to use technology often benefit from professional development opportunities (e.g., seminars, presentations, demonstrations, workshops, summer institutes) that are tailored to their specific instructional or professional interests. When faced with scarce resources and competing choices about supporting computer technology within a department, these teachers may need to be convinced to spend money on technology rather than on other more conventional instructional resources. As a result of their reluctance, these individuals often provide a useful critical perspective or reality check when they are engaged in technology planning efforts. As Teacher/users point out bottlenecks, time constraints, and access issues that can scuttle long-range technology plans, they provide a necessary balance to the often heady projects proposed by Teacher/leaders.

Technical staff—systems administrators and technical coordinators are key participants in a culture of support. Without their help and expertise, it is often impossible to design computer systems designed to support the instructional goals of teachers of English and language arts—systems that allow a range of literacy activities and communication among individuals and groups. Technical staff members—because they often contribute an intimate logistical perspective to discussions of language studies—can also suggest new ways to think about language studies, help conduct research on new software and hardware products, and help teach faculty and students to use applications effectively.

Technical staff members (who may be teachers) are hired to support technology use in a program, department, district, or institution and have an immediate stake in making computer-supported instruction succeed. These individuals—because they have many demands on their time—also have a stake in supporting computer-based instruction and practices that are effective and sustainable over a long period of time. As professionals, they often take great pride in maintaining computer environments that accommodate the instructional needs of teachers and the learning requirements of students. Yet when technical staff are forced or choose to work alone—without regularly communicating with teachers, students, and administrators—they can also allow concerns for systems security, budgetary considerations, and standardization to overwhelm the flexibility and effectiveness of the systems they support.

Technical support professionals can make a huge difference in the culture surrounding technology-rich instruction at all levels if they have they creativity and dedication demonstrated by Joseph Pounds in the following sustainable practice. I constructed this outline of his work after interviewing Joe and collecting many of his online materials. This is an outline of his efforts to creating a culture of support in a K-12 environment. (*Dickie Selfe*).

Attending to Teachers Electronic Needs: A K-12 Support Position

Joseph Pounds
<josephpounds@yahoo.com>
West Noble High School
1-800-488-3191 extension 5027

All the technology-rich programs directed by Joe Pounds (a former high school English teacher, now a Technology Curriculum Specialist) are based on this objective: "Use technology to do something you couldn't do before, or do something you've done before better." For 5 years the program has introduced and supported K-12 teachers in the West Noble School District as they integrate new and established technologies into their classrooms. As a full-time Technology Curriculum Specialist, a person in this type of position works both with the local technology coordinators and the teachers to create professional development opportunities, of course, but also to create curriculum.

For instance, the T.I.M.E. (Technology Integration Made Effective, Easy and Exciting) program is a grant-sponsored effort that recruits teachers who are willing to attend monthly technology workshops with sustained support in between: These teachers, in consultation with Joe Pounds, create new and technology-enhanced curriculum that is sustainable at the local level. Another program at West Noble recognizes the extraordinary time pressure that teachers are under: the time it takes teachers to learn, integrate, and implement new technology-rich activities and curriculum. TimeShare is a new, growing program that encourages community members and parents to plan with teachers and then monitor classroom activities for those teachers attending technology sessions. In addition, Joe has worked to set up regular teacher-led mini-sessions throughout the year, regular conference-like inservices, and a TecHelp hotline.

The technology curriculum specialist (TCS) position also has many institutional responsibilities: Joe Pounds, for instance, helps create technology policy, researches new technologies, acts as a liaison between school, corporate, and community-based "technology advisory bodies (TAB)," and acts as a "change agent" in the district. These TABs involve students, teachers, technology specialists and interested community members in round table discussions that influence policies and budgetary decisions in the district.

In terms of stuff (i.e., fancy Web pages, latest/greatest computers, online education, remediation software, etc.) I don't think you will find us anywhere near above average. Our teachers are not even high-end users. In terms of staff development and staff involvement, however, I feel our school does a cutting-edge job.

Students/Student Workers—too easily categorized only as the end users of technology in classes, students are often overlooked as valuable participants in a departmental culture of support. They come to schools and classrooms with a great deal of formally and informally acquired computer expertise and can serve as assistants and collaborators in computer-supported communication environments. As part of their studies and as part of their service commitment to the school community, students can serve as assistants to technical staff members, consultants to teachers who hold their courses in computer-based classrooms or online environments, research assistants working with teachers who want to acquire technology expertise in particular applications or approaches, and even as collaborators on the design and implementation of technology-rich instruction projects. In computer-supported communication facilities, technical consultants often help recruit and train other student assistants, conduct research on and user test new hardware and software, and provide demonstrations of various applications and programs.

Students who serve in such positions are often supported through independent-study, work-study, internship programs that provide leadership training, and academic credit for projects related to their majors or major areas of study. They can and should be identified and recruited in every technology-rich class taught and encouraged to return to help in the next iteration of that class' computer-supported instruction. In K–12 schools, students often also work in computer-supported classrooms or with computer-using teachers as members of computer clubs or service organizations.

Students are the endusers of teachers' technology-rich instruction. Those who have served in support positions can often provide a great deal of insight into which computer-supported activities worked well in the classroom and how those activities can be modified to be more effective. On departmental technology committees, advanced students can provide input from student constituencies and help conduct surveys to determine how well district-wide, programmatic, or departmental technology efforts meet the needs of students.

Students have multiple reasons for investing in an effective culture of support. Not only do such cultures support innovative teaching—which many students are quick to understand and support—they also provide those students with the opportunity to gain valuable experience using, managing, and even designing technology-rich communication environments. The best cultures of support also provide students a rare opportunity to be experts, help spend budgets, and teach others what they know about using technology in the language arts (e.g., through cross-age tutoring). For many students, this opportunity proves to be a powerful motivating and shaping force in their lives.[2]

Administrators—valuable participants in a culture of support, administrators can help teachers formulate and build important departmental infrastructures to support technology-rich teaching of literacy skills, attitudes, and approaches. Departmental administrators, for example, can help teachers revise tenure, promotion, or performance guidelines so that they recognize teachers' efforts to innovate with technology. They can examine and revise budgeting processes for technology so that they support systematic planning; appoint faculty to college-wide or district-level institutional committees that set technology policies; and communicate with higher level administrators and individuals outside the institution (e.g., legislators, community members, business leaders, parents) who can, in turn, help create and maintain the support for efforts to teach literacy in technological environments.

Different administrators, of course, have different stakes in creating a sustainable culture of support for teaching literacy in electronic environments. For example, most appreciate the importance of providing graduates a range of technological literacy skills and have talked extensively with parents and community members about how best to support technology-rich teaching. Administrators will also appreciate the difficulties associated with funding and assessing technology efforts and appreciate any projects

---

[2]This topic is taken up in more detail in chap. 5.

that provide productive ways to address these challenges. Finally, administrators recognize the difficulties associated with providing adequate technical support, rewarding teachers who work extensively with technology, providing appropriate professional-development opportunities for teachers who want to use technology, and budgeting systematically for ongoing technological change—all projects that an effective culture of support must address.

Other stakeholders—specific institutional and local conditions may also suggest inviting additional participants to join in the effort to form and maintain a culture of support. These individuals might include other institutions, parents, librarians, writing center directors, community members, corporate partners, software and hardware vendors, emeritus and adjunct faculty members, learning specialists, legislative representatives, and distance education specialists. Each of these individuals will contribute specific talents to a team committed to sustaining a culture of support for teaching literacy in technology-rich environments.

The Partnership of the Rhode Island Training School for Youth (RITS) and the Institute for Elementary and Secondary Education (IESE) at Brown University

Judy Williamson, Brown University
<Judy_Williamson@brown.edu>

In 1996, a handful of students from Brown University started a writing and creative arts program for incarcerated youth at the Rhode Island Training School. The presence of Brown University students at the RITS prompted Principal Chorney to initiate a discussion with Brown's Education Department and its in-service, professional development unit, the IESE, about computers and special education at the RITS. Many questions about educational technology emerged, but the primary one that evolved was whether or not the IESE could invest in an ongoing partnership with the RITS instead of offering a series of smaller, separate projects.

Initially, work emphasized solving problems about wires and networks. However, given the IESE mission to pay attention to relationships with teachers, schools, and technologies, we worked to contextualize technology's relationship to teaching and learning, de-emphasizing technology for technology's sake. One result of our work together was the development of an educational technology plan that will guide professional development in the area of technology integration. More important, and more satisfying, however, were broader conversations about educational technology's impact on the ways in which teachers and students work and learn together.

Our work together expanded beyond the walls of the institution when RITS teachers joined other Rhode Island teachers and IESE staff to be part of an AT&T-funded project about culture and diversity where we use the Web for publication. Public, independent, and RITS school teachers have found each others' perspectives and knowledge invaluable in the project, and the inter-change of ideas among schools has created fertile ground for developing ideas and understandings about multicultural issues.

Dr. Chorney has asked IESE staff to join professional development sessions regularly to collaborate with teams on the development of new theme-based curricular units in which technology is a part of the teaching and learning mix. We are also publishing work we developed together—the technology plan, multicultural projects, curricular units, and teaching resources—on the Web.

The Importance of the IESE-RITS Partnership

The challenges of correctional education with incarcerated youth are unlike those experienced by teachers or administrators in any other educational settings. To sustain the partnership, it was essential to recognize that the RITS existed as part of the juvenile justice system in the State of Rhode Island, and it operated under legal mandates. Because the school is embedded in a much more complex system, we needed to recognize constraints and facilitate change in pragmatic ways that acknowledged the realities of teachers and students in a correctional facility.

During the 3-year collaboration, RITS and IESE conversations evolved from concerns about hardware and software decisions to addressing pedagogical transformation that includes technology as just one element in a five-point initiative for educational reform. In addition to educational technology, the other components for change include: an emphasis on literacy; professional development about integration of educational standards into the curriculum; more activities that engage students in the arts; and theme-based, cross-curricular instruction. To support this systemic change, educational technology "will not be a separate curricular entity at the RITS [but will] be integrated into all classroom work" (RITS Ed. Tech. Plan 39). Student needs and student knowledge are more prominent considerations for lesson plans in light of the systemic change Dr. Chorney seeks to implement.

Technological innovation at the RITS is being met with the not-unusual resistance and cynicism of teachers who are asked to enter into a process of change that requires a paradigm shift in their notions about teaching and learning. IESE staff works with teams of teachers as they develop theme-based units — bridges, change, leadership, technology and innovation, positive choices — to offer ideas about integrating technology in ways that support the achievement of educational standards and address other key areas for improving teaching and learning at the RITS.

Sustaining the Partnership

To sustain this partnership, it was essential to build trust and credibility with teachers who had seen many outsiders come and go who wanted to "help." It was also essential to work with RITS teachers as partners, to recognize the dedication, knowledge, and talents they bring to their students. We had to abandon the position of "outside expert" and learn to listen, and to observe, offering our expertise as a contribution to collaborative work, not as a prescriptive solution to a task or problem.

Not inconsequential was the need for those of us who came from the university to examine our own cultural notions as we entered the locked gates of this facility. How, for example, did we view the students and teachers in a prison? To interact with them in any significant way, we needed to recognize our own cultural assumptions about prisons, and what kind of schooling juvenile offenders could receive. Facilitating change would have been impossible if we had not taken time to understand and value the unique qualities of the institution, which is remarkably progressive and successful given its constraints.

Follow-Up Resources
Main partnership home page:
 <http://www.brown.edu/IESE/RITS/>
Educational Technology Plan:
 <http://www.brown.edu/IESE/RITS/edtech>

Is an extensive team of people really needed to sustain a culture of support for teaching English, composition, and language arts in technological environments? For long-term support, I'd say "Yes." Typically, only 5 % to 10 % of a faculty population are willing or able to take on the role of technology leader in a department at any one point in time. Unfortunately, sustainable programs cannot thrive for long on such an exclusive membership. Nor are sustainable efforts often initiated and maintained exclusively by administrative fiat—such an approach typically generates some level of resentment and resistance and can exacerbate a local dynamic of blame, rather than encourage committed action on the part of teachers.

A successful culture will provide support not only to faculty willing to lead technology efforts but faculty who are more cautious in their integration of computer-supported instruction; and it will involve, as well, a range of individuals who have a stake in providing effective technology-rich literacy instruction and who can contribute their talents to sustaining such an effort.

SUCCESSFUL CULTURES OF SUPPORT

What does a culture of support look like? What activities does such a culture contain? I have hinted at answers to these questions, and I certainly cannot outline a specific culture of support for every kind of institution. Yet I can identify some common components of such cultures worth working toward:

- A team of interested stakeholders to meet on a regular basis.
- A team of teacher/leaders who are supported in their efforts and involved in shaping the culture of support.
- Robust and flexible digital environments that support the day-to-day activities of teachers.
- A Student Technology Assistant (STA) Program in which students support teachers in technology-rich projects.
- Workshops led by teachers of English and language arts that contextualize technology use specifically within the scope of English and language arts instruction.
- Robust and flexible computer-supported environments designed specifically to support English and language arts classes.

Supporting Stakeholders Teams

In most programs, it is a rare moment when representatives from a range of groups meet and talk about the needs of English and language arts teachers engaged in technology-rich instruction. These types of activities do not develop entirely on their own, and schools that want to develop a culture of support need to establish a systematic effort to make them happen on a regular basis, providing help in identifying the members of such teams, assistance in setting up a regular schedule for such meetings, and offering the space needed for such meetings.

Supporting Teacher/Leaders

For most programs, the centerpiece of a culture of support consists of this team of teachers, administrators, students, and technical staff members committed to supporting and sustaining technology efforts in support of the teaching of literacy. However, because the efforts of such a team focuses on the teaching and learning of literacy, the core leadership and motivation often depends on the willing and enthusiastic involvement of one or more English and language arts teachers. These are often individuals who are early adopters of technology, but they are also committed and talented teachers who want to support the efforts of other teachers and students to practice communication in meaningful ways in technological environments.

Recruiting and supporting these colleagues over time is often a difficult task. If teachers commit to the extra work and demands placed on them to teach with technology and take leadership roles constructing cultures of support at their institutions, their work should be valued in visible ways. Unfortunately, such work is relatively new, and those individuals who have the most to say about job descriptions and "what counts" as valued work have not had to face the challenges of teacher/leaders: those senior colleagues, for instance, in teachers' unions, on school boards, hiring committees, and tenure and promotion committees. In addition, institutional measuring tools are not built to accommodate a type of teaching that is inherently experimental and risky.

To address this situation, new job descriptions, methods of salary adjustment, systems of release time, changed responsibilities, and faculty assessment systems are going to have to be put in place to provide more visible ways of valuing the technology-rich efforts suggested in this volume[3] Moreover, teacher leaders will have to undertake the task of educating administrators and their colleagues about what kinds of time and effort are involved for teacher/leaders in supporting a sustainable program of technology use among teachers of English and language arts; administering computer-supported labs, classrooms, and online environments; serving on institutional committees that make technology policy and decision; offering professional-development opportunities; or taking responsibility for assembling a team of stakeholders responsible for innovative efforts to teach and learn with technology.

Supporting Robust and Flexible Digital Environments for the Day-to-Day Work of Teachers

If technology teachers/leaders in English and language arts are going to be comfortable in digital environments, they have to be able to conduct daily business in those environments. In determining whether any given department's or institution's computer environments are sufficiently robust and flexible for such work, the following questions are useful:

- Are faculty and staff machines reliably upgraded and connected to the WWW?
- Do English and language arts faculty have adequate and appropriate access from classes, labs, offices, their home, and the library?
- Are there faculty/staff technology support persons who work primarily with teachers, often on instructional projects?
- Are there student technology support persons—those who direct facilities, administer computer systems, and facilitate improved efforts to teach with technology?
- Are faculty working in safe, convenient, and appropriate digital environments in the classroom, in labs, online, at home, in libraries, or via community centers?
- Do clerical support staff conduct departmental business online?
- Is some (or most) departmental school business conducted on computers (with additional kinds of accommodative support for individuals who cannot or will not otherwise participate)?

---

[3]For an example of how college-level English studies professionals are trying to change the culture of promotion and tenure, see Cindy Selfe's case studies at < http://www.hu.mtu.edu/ ~ cyselfe/P&Tstuff/P&Tweb/introduction.htm > and the associated links to the NCTE and MLA technology and tenure statements.

- Do institutional and departmental chairs participate on administrative e-mail lists and in WWW environments when appropriate?
- Is there appropriate travel and professional development moneys for academics and staff willing to upgrade their technological skills?

The ideal answers to these questions are, of course, goals toward which a department or institution might work over time. They all cost money, and those costs have to be balanced against other interests. Yet they are not always an "add on" to the current responsibilities of schools and teachers. For instance, if concerns about diversity of access and the digital divide are a departmental or institutional priority (cf. Selfe, 1999), some of the issues mentioned earlier may already be central to a school's culture rather than an additional enhancement.

There is one caveat for those who are implementing or are ready to begin implementing these day-to-day levels of involvement. One might expect day-to-day involvement with communication technologies to give faculty and staff enough confidence to incorporate them into their course planning. However, that type of transfer does not always take place naturally or quickly. English and language arts teachers who are often trained in more conventional programs of English studies, for instance, may not value classroom-based involvement with computer technology and, thus, may not choose to take the time out of their busy professional lives needed for making the connections between their own changing digital work habits and the possible curricular innovations that they might apply to their classes.

In other words, it will not do simply to supply teachers of English and language arts with digital working environments. A culture of support will, on a regular basis, explore the explicit connections between our changing professional literacy practices and the way we teach our students. A useful workshop outline for this purpose might look like the following:

- Begin by asking teachers to list the literacy skills, attitudes, and approaches needed for students (and for themselves) to be literate citizens in the 21st century.
- Discuss how new communication technologies are (or are not) changing the medium in which professionals correspond or the way they compose their materials for publication or presentation (online or in print).
- Discuss how these skills and attitudes might be reinforced in specific classes as students research and collect information,

synthesize and evaluate information, and compose and distribute reports, papers, and new media presentations.

Supporting a Student Technology Assistants (STA) Program

Teachers consistently report that what they most need—as they try to stay abreast of both their content areas and changing communication technologies—is desk-side support for their technology-rich instructional efforts. To support teachers in this way, departments of English and language arts, local technology coordinators, faculty senates, and instructional technology departments can create training programs that pay talented students to work with teachers in developing innovative, technology-rich projects. Institution-wide STA programs seem like an ideal solution, but English and language arts departments need not wait for the university or K–12 bureaucracies to adopt this effort. The following first three options are available to every department with willing participants. The fourth represents a campus-wide initiative that is gaining acceptance across the nation:

- *Independent-study programs:* Talented students interested in becoming teaching assistants can be recruited for technology-rich projects or classes on the basis of independent study credit for their work.
- *Volunteer student-run workshops for professional development:* The director of technology-rich labs, classrooms, centers, and virtual environments at an institution may be willing to encourage student staff members working in those sites to design and carry out workshops for English and language arts faculty or assist faculty in carrying out the workshops. Often students can be rewarded for their involvement with letters of recommendation, expanded access to technology, independent study credits, or some voice in spending technology funds.
- *Programmatic integration:* Integrate technology training for students into curricular programs. Students who encounter technology in one class can then work with teachers of other classes who want to develop technology-rich projects. Joe Essid and Dona Hickey at the University of Richmond, for instance, have folded technology support into the training they conduct for students in their English major. Those students then go out into the university and work with teachers who are incorporating writing and communicating into other courses. That training is one

thread that English majors at their institution can choose. At Michigan Technological University, technical communication undergraduate and graduate students who are interested in instructional design can run technology workshops for faculty as part of their program.

- *Paid and Trained STAs:* Working with other departments or other units on campus (like the library), some English and language arts programs are able to establish institution-wide STA programs. To see and read about an excellent model for this type of program, take a look at my colleagues' Web page at < http://www.uwm.edu/IMT/STS/stspages/aboutSTS.html. More examples and sites are listed in chapter 5.

Supporting Workshops That Contextualize Technology Use Specifically Within English and Language Arts Instruction

Teachers generally do not benefit from workshops based on a "technology inoculation" model. They do, however, report benefits from workshops that contextualize instruction in familiar disciplinary frameworks. Departments that offer a robust culture of support encourage technology workshop leaders to ask and answer the following questions before they design workshops: "What can or should teachers of English language arts *do* with these computer applications/programs/ machines/systems and why?" "What do they currently *want* to do?"

   Unfortunately, in departments that lack a culture of support for teachers who use computers, this question is rarely asked. More commonly, leaders of technology workshops simply ask, "What can these systems do?" This approach often characterizes workshops involving demonstrations of course-authoring software like Blackboard or WebCT, which focus on the options and menu items that the programs provide. In contrast, a contextualized workshop might ask workshop coordinators to tailor the activities to the actual projects that English and language arts teachers are already planning and implementing. Contextualized workshops might also provide time for teachers to review the main options of the technology in question, but their primary objective would be to provide individuals with time to work on the projects they are currently developing—surrounded by supportive technicians (students, professionals, parents, and Teacher/ leaders).

   The timing and duration of such workshops, seminars, brown-bag sessions, or institutes is also crucial and highly contextual. Because communication technologies never stop changing and because technology-rich instructional designs are inherently exploratory, a program, department, or institution can never have too many work-shopping opportunities. The following options represent just a few of the models successful schools use for scheduling workshops. Readers should consider combining and sequencing these categories around topic areas of local interest.

- Weekly meetings: informal, self-determining workshops that alternate between hands-on work and discussions of theory and classroom practice, with weekly meeting notes disseminated throughout the school, college, or department.
- Multiple-day workshops each term that might include surveying teachers about their needs and interests, letting those needs and interests determine workshop topics, recruiting students or other professionals who can lead and support hands-on demonstrations and practice, and planning for plenty of supported, project-based work time.
- Yearly paid or supported attendance for key individuals at annual intensive, extended institutes. If providing this sort of experience locally seems unfeasible, look for institutes suitable for key individuals in your program on the WWW. (See examples from Michigan Technological University, "Computers In Writing Intensive Classes" (CIWIC) at < http://www.hu.mtu. edu/ciwic > and "Electronic Communication Across the Curriculum in K–12" at < http://www.hu.mtu.edu/ecac > .) The criteria suggested earlier might be useful in choosing from among institutes or workshops. The summer institutes held at Michigan Tech, for instance, currently focus on different English studies audiences (compositionists, new media specialists, and local K–12 teachers from across the curriculum).

Supporting Robust and Flexible Computer-Supported Environments Specifically Designed to Support English and Language Arts Classes

Many successful cultures of support centered around some form of computer-supported teaching and learning environment designed and operated to serve the needs of English and language arts classes. These environments can be entirely online, or they can consist of some combination of physical site and online space. The navigational and technical complexity of these online or onsite environments in educational institutions is increasing as English and language arts teachers gain expertise with computer-supported communication.

For instance, it is not unusual these days to find an English studies or language arts course supported by an assemblage of online e-tools that form a teaching and learning environment. These spaces, may offer "home-grown" course management tools (such as Clemson's Collaborative Learning Environment or Texas Tech's TOPIC) or commercial versions of these packages (such as WebCT or Blackboard, local e-mail services or free Web & mail services, online assessment and portfolio systems (such as the University of Texas' Learning Record Online), Web page development spaces that can be accessed locally or at a distance, all manner of local file transfer and management systems, and an amazing array of course content Web sites scattered around the Internet. These complex systems support both professional development efforts for teachers and computer-based classes for students.

Physical environments for computer-supported teaching and learning—labs, classrooms, and centers designed for teachers of English and language arts—have also become quite complex. Some are dedicated entirely to the teaching of language arts and staffed with professional teachers, technical support staff, and student assistants. Many of these facilities are networked, through a campus backbone, to the Internet and to the desktop machines of individual faculty members. Often such facilities contain a range of word processing, graphics, page layout, new media, digital photography, and Web authoring software to support the teaching of English and language arts through the creation of both conventional texts and new-media texts. Adding to this complexity of such sites in K–12 schools are facilities that house teachers and students from several disciplines to share interdisciplinary facilities sometimes located in a library or learning center.

The most successful cultures of support maintain robust online and onsite environments and computer-supported facilities by involving teams of individuals who have an interested stake in their operation. These representatives meet on a regular basis and contribute insight and energy to the management of such facilities, the creation of technology policies that shape what goes on in these teaching and learning spaces, and the decision making involved in the daily operation of such facilities—including decisions about hardware and software purchases, security, staffing, hours of operation, and the best ways to meet the needs of users with the available resources. This topic is taken up in more detail in chapter 3.

CHAPTER CONCLUSION

This chapter makes a case for involving interested stakeholders from across the educational landscape in all sustainable technology-rich instructional systems or environments. Strangely, English studies teachers—partly because of their humanist educations and leanings, and partly because of the ubiquity of computing and telecommunication systems in our culture—often seem to prefer that computer systems for supporting their efforts remain invisible, something to be attended to by others. However, it will become increasingly important during the next decade for humanist educators to understand their responsibility for actively designing and shaping these systems. Such systems have a vast potential to reconfigure the working, teaching, and learning environments of literacy professionals and their students. Technicians and technical support people are not in the best position, to understand how these changes will alter the teaching of English and language arts.

Robert Johnson begins his book, *User-Centered Technology: A Rhetorical Theory for Computers and Other Mundane Artifacts*, with an apropos quote from Aristotle:

> . . . the user, or in other words, the master, of the house will even be a better judge than the builder, just as the pilot will judge better of the rudder than the carpenter, and the guest will judge better of the feast than the cook.
>
> *Politica*

(quoted in Johnson, p. 3)

Teachers are the users of technology-rich instructional systems and spaces. We are the better judges of their design. The following chapter takes up this type of planning and involvement in more detail by outlining and explaining a process that can be adapted to many institutional contexts. Before moving on, however, readers might want to look into the remarkable, pedagogy-based team work of Michael Palmquist and the folks at Colorado State University.

An Integrated, Writing Center-Based, Technology Support Approach to Writing Across the Curriculum at Colorado State University (and isn't that a mouthful?)

Michael Palmquist <Mike.Palmquist@ColoState.edu>
Colorado State University

For more than a decade, we have been developing an alternative to the top-down (I might say, "trickle-down") approach to writing-across-the-curriculum (WAC). The top-down approach, which has been used at many institutions with great success, is characterized by outreach from WAC specialists, usually in the form of seminars, to disciplinary faculty who subsequently use writing in their courses. Until the early 1990s, in fact, we had used this approach at our institution. Unfortunately, our efforts failed to help us win the hearts, minds, and class time of more than a handful of disciplinary writing faculty.

In the spring of 1993, we assembled a 12-person team and spent the following academic year intensely studying how writing was used at our institution in one discipline–electrical engineering. We asked faculty about their perceptions of student writing abilities and about the reasons they did–or did not–use writing in their courses; we asked students about their experiences with writing in their courses and their perceptions of its likely role in their professional lives; we conducted a workplace study of recent EE graduates and interviewed the people who hired and supervised them; and we conducted a national survey of how electrical engineers used writing in their professional lives.

The results of our study surprised us. Many of our assumptions about the kinds of writing used in the electrical engineering curriculum and in the workplace proved unfounded. Perhaps most important, however, we learned, as many WAC scholars have noted, that the single most important barrier to a successful WAC program at our university was our faculty–or, perhaps more accurately, the reward structure that informed their decisions about whether to use writing in their courses. Given the choice of spending 40 hours assigning, responding to, and grading a writing assignment in their courses or spending that same 40 hours writing a grant proposal or article, the faculty would reasonably choose the activity that would have the biggest impact on a favorable performance review–and, at our research university, that choice was seldom the writing assignment.

However, we also learned that faculty were willing to use writing-to-learn and writing-in-the-disciplines assignments in their courses if they could do so in a way that would take somewhat less time away from their research activities. As a result, we began working on a four-track strategy. First, we continued faculty outreach through one-on-one work with disciplinary faculty and faculty seminars. Second, we expanded our WAC outreach efforts to include direct instruction and tutoring of students, following Tori Haring-Smith's "bottom-up" approach to WAC. Third, we created a more visible center for writing instruction at the University by housing our WAC program in our Writing Center. Finally, we worked through college, university, and faculty council committees to restructure the rewards system at our University.

We have enjoyed strong success in the first three tracks and have made surprising headway in the fourth. Our "integrated approach" to WAC has resulted in the creation of a significant collection of instructional materials housed in our Online Writing Center (http://writing. colostate.edu). Our Writing Center, formerly directed by a temporary lecturer, is now directed by a tenure-track faculty member (funded through permanent funding for our WAC program allocated by our Provost), who is also our WAC director. More important, the Writing Center has become so visible on campus that we are finding it difficult to meet demand for its services. Finally, changes to our faculty evaluation procedures, thanks to timely changes approved by our Faculty Council (and abetted by one of our faculty, who chaired our Committee on Teaching and Learning), have increased the rewards for teaching, which has in many departments reduced faculty resistance to using writing in their courses.

In addition to the Online Writing Center, our WAC program has also brought into existence two other online resources. Academic. Writing: Interdisciplinary Perspectives on Communication Across the Curriculum (http://aw.colostate.edu) and The Online Writing Center Consortium (http://owcc.colostate.edu) provide support for faculty at our university and beyond.

3

PLANNING TECHNOLOGY-RICH ENVIRONMENTS

SUMMARY OF TOPICS

▶ Reflecting on beauty in cyborg environments (p. 56)
▶ Following a user-centered design process for computer-rich environments that supports real teachers and learners (p. 58)

Step 1: Identify the instructional needs of students (p. 59)
Step 2: Articulate explicit pedagogical goals based on teachers' understanding of students' needs (p. 59)
Step 3: Operationalize pedagogical goals through technologies, environments, systems, and people (p. 59)
Step 4: Continue to build and change computer-rich environments from a position of strength (p. 59

▶ A case study of user-centered design: valuing collaboration (p. 74)
▶ The following chapters (p. 82)

This chapter describes and provides some justification for a process—a method of designing technology-rich environments that is user-centered and flexible enough to address the needs of teachers and students from a wide range of English studies and language arts programs across the country. A key characteristic of this process is that it begins with human beings.

The first two steps of the process discuss how to focus on the communication needs of students in English and language arts classes and how to derive from these needs a set of instructional or pedagogical goals in which a broad range of faculty can invest. The third step of the process discusses how to operationalize these goals—choosing computer technologies that help people accomplish their goals, shaping computer-rich environments and systems in which people can pursue their goals. The fourth and final step of the process addresses how to continue building and enriching such environments, working from a position of professional and intellectual strength. In all steps of the design process, the chapter encourages teachers of English and language arts to work with students, technical support staff, and others who have a stake in making computer-supported teaching and learning environments useful places.

The intention in this chapter is not to describe a single rigidly detailed planning process that will lead all English and language arts programs to create the same ideal technology-rich environment or system. Such an environment—such a system—does not exist. Rather, this chapter supports the claim that designing effective computer-supported teaching and learning environments is a rhetorically sophisticated task that must be taken up by colleagues embedded in—and thus cognizant of—local technical, social, and educational conditions. As the social theorist Anthony Giddens (1979) said, "every social actor knows a great deal about the conditions of reproduction of the society of which he or she is a member" (p. 5) and can apply this understanding to the task of shaping social systems in productive ways. Technology-rich environments give educators and other stakeholders unusual opportunities to shape teaching and learning systems. When they become participatory designers of these systems, they also have the opportunity to shape English studies and language arts curricula in new and innovative ways.

WORKING WITH HEART, AS WELL AS HEAD AND HANDS

Technology-rich environments tend to be characterized by change—they are either new or being redesigned. However, the *exact* trajectory and pace of development—the nature of change—within specific technology-rich educational environments is such a complicated affair that it is hard to know where to look or put one's energy to effect change. These spaces exist as complex cyborg systems in which technologies, institutions, and people interact and shape one another.

In fact it may be essential not only to appreciate and pay attention to this complexity, but to value it and appreciate the beauty inherent in the complicated mixture. This is true whether a program, department, or institution is starting from scratch to develop a new computer-supported teaching and learning environment or trying to reinvigorate an existing environment. Bonnie Nardi and Vicky O'Day provided us with a useful way to think about the complex beauty of technology-rich teaching and learning environments. In their chapter "How to Evolve Information Ecologies," found in *Information Ecologies: Using Technology with Heart,* Nardi and O'Day suggested the following:

> We have been urging readers to get more involved in their local information ecologies. We believe that there are some practical ways to do this effectively. They can be summarized as follows:
>
> - Work from core values . . . work with heart, as well as the head and hands.
> - Pay attention. Notice what meanings are assigned to technologies as they are used, or intended to be used, in your ecology. Reflect aloud about what you notice.
> - Ask strategic, open-ended questions about use. Perform thought experiments by asking "what-if" questions along the way.
>
> There is a Zen saying that, roughly paraphrased, embodies this interesting idea: when you consider an object, it is what you see that makes the object beautiful and what you don't see that makes it useful. (p. 65)

The process sketched out in this chapter attends to Nardi and O'Day's suggestions. It encourages English and language arts teachers to practice seeing the beauty and meaning of technology-rich environments and to ask themselves public, open-ended questions that will help mold these digital communication systems into sustainable cyborg environments. To illustrate this process, I offer readers the following glimpse of the complex beauty inherent in the computer-rich teaching and learning environment that I inhabit on a daily basis—the Center for Computer-Assisted Language Instruction—a facility that serves the Department of Humanities at Michigan Technological University (MTU).

REFLECTIONS ON A CYBORG ENVIRONMENT

It is rare to see or hear English studies and language arts educators reflect on the beauty and usefulness of computer-supported teaching and learning environments. This is partially because we have the habit of understanding them in a limited way—as if they are classrooms, spaces filled with computers or as if they are only virtual spaces created within a computer system. When we take this perspective, however, we often fail to recognize that these environments are made up of both people and machines, and we fail to acknowledge the dynamic interactions through which humans and computers influence each other within such spaces as they comprise living cyborg systems. When we can learn to appreciate these cyborg systems, to see their complex beauty, we gain valuable motivation for paying attention to the goals that shape them and the daily, technical decision making that sustains them. It is at these moments that technology-rich teaching and learning environments can surprise and even delight us.

When I walk into the Center for Computer-Assisted Language Instruction (CCLI), it is the students who first attract attention—they are responsive to each other as they chat about classes, assignments, teachers, and life outside of school. They work alone, talk across the computers, gather in groups at the printers, and respond to instant messages from friends across campus or the world. They are also in constant communication with the machines—using e-mail, playing games online, staring at screens on which seven or eight different applications are open, and active in the service of a single communication project. Teachers occupy this space, too, sometimes using the machines, sometimes working with individuals in their classes. Lab consultants—undergraduate and graduate students—circulate in the interstices of the social space answering questions, working on projects, and providing support and expertise.

The machines, too, are hard to miss. Seldom entirely clean, always well used, and constantly in need of upgrading, they flash login prompts, glow patiently, and offer glimpses of photographs, movies, pages of text, games, pulsing audio signatures, and color palettes. They communicate with each other through snaking cables and with the students via the reflected light from screens or the mechanical click of keyboards. Those that sit unused wait for the next student, the next teacher, the next class that comes through the door.

In this space, the arrangement of the room as well as the careful placement of peripherals encourage some activities and discourage others. Wall hangings, student art, the refrigerator, and the microwave oven encourage students, teachers, technicians, and visitors to populate these rooms. The telephone, arm chairs, and mailboxes make the space social, and hospitable. The arrangement of tables in pods leaves little room for privacy. The actions of humans and the presence of machines, then, are familiar, well known, and comfortable—even when the sharper urgency of an overdue project or the confusion of a new class interrupts a more constant hum.

Underneath the humans and the machines, the printers and the conversation, is a remarkably complex network system—UNIX, Macintosh, and Windows—that draws on local human and electrical energy and sends packets of information from person to person, office to office, and place to place. This is a connected place—the room connected to the campus backbone, the campus connected to the state network, the state network linked rhizomatically to the national information infrastructure, the Web. This network of machines connects students and teachers in the CCLI to family members, grandparents who send e-mail, friends at other institutions, and chatroom correspondents who exchange information about gardening, games, indie music groups, and so on.

On good days, these humans and technical systems interact productively, together, constituting a wonderful synergistic dance—a choreographed ensemble of effort and ability. The noises and activity that attend this dance indicate that "communities of practice" are forming: "tight-knit groups formed . . . by people working together on the same of similar tasks" (Brown & Duguid, p. 141). As Brown and Duguid suggested, these communities are the anvils on which most useable knowledge and learning—social and practical—is hammered out. The digital space we provide enables a wider "reach" for these groups as they work onsite and at a distance. Hence, the CCLI becomes one of the places on campus where these little communities of practice form and reform. We need to appreciate our part in providing for this essential component of students' curricular and self-directed learning.

My guess is that the energetic beauty of the CCLI and other computer-rich facilities—to most people and at most times—is invisible. I suspect they would prefer that it remain that way. At appropriate moments, however, the designers and stewards of these environments—the English/language arts teachers who use and administer them, as well as the students and technology specialists who make them work—need to savor the complex sophistication of the systems they have helped create and the conditions that keep them going. Without these rare moments of reflection, the difficulty of ongoing analysis, research, refinement, retooling, and fiscal decision making will take its toll.

The Seen and the Unseen

If *paying attention* to the complexity and beauty of cyborg environments is difficult, *understanding what is not there*—what Nardi and O'Day said makes an environment *useful*—is even harder.

One way to interpret this comment about usefulness concerns the many digital and physical spaces we have left for teachers and students to fill in and around these environments. These spaces are "not there" until they become occupied by people, working groups, classes, and teachers and students. In part, the health of a technology-rich teaching and learning environment can be gauged by the number, depth, and breadth of these unfilled spaces; by the amount and kinds of activities and personalities and initiatives they will hold—initiatives that are student-centered, teacher-centered, technician-centered, institutionally-centered.

Another way to think about *what is not there* has to do with a question that might be asked by Donald Norman (1989): "What *could* such an environment afford its users that it does not yet do?" This act requires an imaginative leap in time—it requires literacy professionals and students to think of themselves as agents, individuals able to enact productive change in and around computer-rich environments through some sort of strategic and concerted action.

The complex beauty of computer-rich environments, in other words— exists in their accessibility—physically and imaginatively—to students, teachers, and administrators who use, inhabit, maintain, and re-create them day by day, week by week, term by term, year after year. The beauty—like the environments—is cyborg in nature, not human alone and not computer alone. Entirely interdependent, it has to do with a human endeavor, but one that unfolds within, and depends on, a technological context.

A User-Centered Design Process

English and language arts educators now have more than 20 years of experience in creating and sustaining electronic environments for teaching and learning. Even when personal computers first came on the educational scene in 1979, pioneering teachers understood that such environments could prove to be valuable additions to the classroom instruction in their departments. Of course not all the digital environments that teachers established since that time have fulfilled this promise, nor have they all represented sustainable efforts over the long run. Indeed far too many computer-supported teaching and learning environments have been established with excellent intentions and at great cost only to be used infrequently or to become quickly obsolete and abandoned. Often this situation occurs when computer-rich environments have been designed from the perspective of only one group of people—technical support staff, for instance, who may not understand how faculty members' goals could shape a teaching and learning environment; or teachers, for instance, who may not understand how students' needs might shape such environments.

The most successful computer-supported environments for English and language arts, however, now have a 20-year history of supporting instruction in programs, departments, and institutions. Computer-rich teaching and learning systems work best—as it turns out—when they are committed to supporting the changing needs of a wide range of students and the changing instructional goals of a wide range of faculty. They also work best when the process of their design—and continual reassessment and redesign (see chap. 5)—involves those people who have a stake in their operation: students, teachers, and technical support staff, in particular, and administrators and others, more generally.

The task of designing such an environment, as we have said, is ongoing—teachers in charge of such an endeavor are either designing a new environment from scratch or designing new features that will accommodate changing teaching and learning needs. In either case, however, the design team for such environments should include teachers, students, and technical support staff who can provide input from a variety of perspectives and in a variety of forms (as detailed in chap. 2). Further, the starting point for design efforts should be the same:

Step 1: Identify the instructional needs of students.

Step 2: Articulate the pedagogical goals of English/language arts teachers.

Step 3: Operationalize the instructional goals through technologies, environments, systems, and people.

Step 4: Build and change computer-rich environments from a position of strength as we learn and as technologies and instructional needs change.

The sections that follow explain each of these steps more fully.

Step 1: Identify the Instructional Needs of Students. One of the most valuable aspects of designing a computer-based teaching and learning environment is that such an effort can provide an opportunity—some even consider it an excuse—for English and language arts teachers to re-examine the needs of students in light of rapidly changing cultural communication contexts.

Among the questions that literacy professionals may want to use as guidance for such an effort are the following:

- What literacies—that is, what literacy skills and values—do students bring to the table in their English/language arts classes within this program? Department? Institution?
- What specific literacy problems—research, reading, writing, composing problems—do students exhibit within English/language arts classes?
- What future literacy skills and values, and understandings will students need to be active and productive citizens in the increasingly technological communication contexts that will undoubtedly characterize the next decade?

Some faculties find it useful to respond to these questions as a community of professionals. If this is an initial effort, it is often conducted during a series of shorter faculty meetings or in a longer retreat where faculty brainstorm a locally specific list of students' instructional needs. The following lists of students' literacy needs (Fig. 3.1), for instance, were gathered during brainstorming sessions at MTU's annual summer institute on computer-supported literacy:

In such meetings, some English and language arts teachers also find it useful to consult state and national professional standards that have identified the communication needs of citizens in coming decades. In the English and Language Arts Content Standards published jointly by the National Council of Teachers of English and the International Reading Association, for instance, the following statements may prove to be a valuable focus for discussion and debate:

> To take advantages of the resources that technology offers and to become prepared for the demands that will face them in the future, students need to learn how to use an array of technologies, from computers and computer networks, to electronic mail, interactive video, and CD-ROM. . . . Students should use computers, then, to compose texts and graphics for themselves and others and to publish their own works. This requires skill in keyboarding and word-processing as stu-

STUDENT WRITING CHALLENGES

- low self-confidence w/ regard to writing
- weak reading muscles – esp. conventional genre
- too high an opinion/resentment
- difference of opinion about what writing is
- there is only one way of writing
- take critique personally
- lang. is personal – students don't understand
- teachers' assumptions/recog. of diff. needs
- unpacking academic texts – idea 2nd concept
- figuring out what teachers want
- different literacies/comm. patterns
- resistance to editing/discussing writing
- in revision, focusing on word-by-word
- strategies for revision
- analyze & tying into to purpose/context (especially historical)
- learning how to read texts
- developing critical consciousness
- words – identity – culture
- critique vs. coach
- 5 p → longer works
- rhetoric – understand
- lack vocab.
- organizational strategies
- logical strategies
- lack understanding of privilege/context of privilege

Figure 3.1 A List of Student Literacy Needs Compiled by One of the English/Language Arts Teachers.

dents draft, revise, and edit their writing, seeking feedback from peers and teachers along the way. Students should use computers individually and collaboratively to develop and publish a variety of works such as storybooks, essays, newsletters, classroom anthologies, and school newspapers. Also extended use of computers should be encouraged when connection to a network makes it possible to correspond with others nearby or far away. (Standards for the *English Language Arts*, 1996, pp. 39–40)

In other cases—especially when a faculty has already worked as a group to identify students' needs as the starting point for some other curricular effort such as a writing-across-the-curriculum program—existing lists of students' needs can be updated in shorter discussions held on a periodic basis. This is often the case for programs and departments that already have a technology-rich teaching and learning environment and use the task of regularly identifying students' needs to update the focus and priorities of such an environment. In either case, the broader the level of participation in this activity, the more often it happens, and the more accurate the list of students' needs it yields, the more likely it is that faculty members with different priorities and interests will invest in the planning efforts that follow.

It is important that students be involved at this stage of design, too. In fact any list of students' literacy needs should be considered incomplete until students themselves have contributed their own special perspective to this task.

Step 2: Articulate a set of pedagogical goals based on teachers' understanding of students' needs. The next step in the planning process for technology-rich environments involves English/language arts teachers articulating a broadly inclusive set of programmatic goals based on their shared understanding of students' literacy needs. To guide their efforts in compiling such a list, faculty members may find the following questions useful:

- Given the instructional needs of students enrolled in this program, what broad pedagogical goals should be our focus?
- Based on what we know about the teaching of English and language arts, what broad pedagogical goals should be shaping our classroom and pedagogical efforts?

The following list of goals (Fig. 3.2) were formulated as a basis for MTU's computer-supported environment, the CCLI. These goals are posted in the facility so that faculty and students can offer their input and suggestions for revision on an ongoing basis.

These goals—as the next section explains—were also used by teachers and students who work in the CCLI as a touchstone for making explicit operational decisions about priorities in the purchase of hardware and software, staffing, hours of operation, professional development of staff, and ambiance.

CCLI INSTRUCTIONAL GOALS

Goal #1 Encourage students to practice communicating as often as possible and to improve their skill as communicators.

Goal #2 Support the concept of communicating for a variety of purposes, using a variety of communication strategies, aiming for a variety of audiences.

Goal #3 Promote a socially situated, process-based approach to communication.

Goal #4 Help students recognize that all communication takes place with—and is shaped by—social and political contexts, and that communication can help individuals and groups enact/encourage social change.

Goal #5 Encourage collaborative exchanges among communicators and teachers of communication: peer feedback, student-teacher conferences, individual practice with communication.

Goal #6 Support effective process-based communication instruction for students and teachers who request it: communication-intensive classes, conferences, individual practice with communication.

Goal #7 Help communicators learn to be critical readers of their own and others' communications.

Goal #8 Encourage communicators to learn and share successful strategies.

Figure 3.2 Instructional Goals for MTU's CCLI.

This approach of identifying instructional goals for technology-rich environments encourages teachers to articulate a set of shared pedagogical values in which a broad range of faculty can invest; it also provides a set of shared guidelines for creating an environment that mirrors the instructional goals a faculty considers important and students will find useful. In this way, the approach can help encourage broad support for a computer-supported environment within a program, department, or institution. In addition, when faculty have listened to what students have said about the challenges of literacy, instruction benefits from being increasingly relevant to a particular student population. Finally—as the next section indicates—this list of general instructional goals can serve as a valuable basis for making operational decisions in a computer-supported teaching and learning facility.

The planning process suggested in this chapter is based largely on the workshop process developed over the years at our summer institutes.

Summer Workshops in the Humanities Department of Michigan Technological University. Houghton, Michigan

Cindy Selfe, Dickie Selfe, & Anne Wysocki

* Computers in Writing-Intensive Classrooms (CIWIC, AIC and NM)

* Electronic Communication Across the Curriculum in K-12 (ECAC)

—CIWIC, AIC <http://www.hu.mtu.edu/ciwic/aic/contents.html>—

The first of these three summer workshops is CIWIC, Approaches to Integrating Computers (AIC). It has been under the direction of Cindy Selfe for 17 years and is self supporting. It provides a 2-week institute for English studies and language arts teachers who want to incorporate computers into their writing-intensive courses and/or programs. The workshop is held in a fully equipped, state-of-the-art computer facility designed especially for such teachers (The Center for Computer-Assisted Language Instruction [CCLI]). Participants have the opportunity to survey the research conducted in this field and to think about both the theory and practice of integrating technology into writing-intensive classes. They do this as they are introduced to and use an array of technologies and systems.

—*CIWIC, NW* <http://www.hu.mtu.edu/ciwic/nm/contents. html>

For 2 years, under the expert direction of Anne Wysocki, we have offered CIWIC, New Media (NM). Participants develop approaches to teaching the interpretation and development of new media texts within writing-intensive classrooms and programs. Through the process of composing their own multimedia texts (with plenty of cheery and thoughtful hands-on assistance), participants consider how compositional and rhetorical approaches to writing carry over into the interactive and intensely visual places of computer screens. This workshop is also based in the CCLI.

In addition to regularly scheduled sessions, the CCLI is opened and staffed during the evenings to both AIC and NM participants. All participants receive one-on-one help in learning and developing curricula using computer applications suited to their own classrooms and programs. In addition, all participants may choose to receive 3 hours of graduate credit.

Its success year after year is due primarily to the substantial human support provided to participants by student consultants, graduate student assistant directors, the workshop organizers (Drs. Cindy Selfe and Anne Wysocki), and the participants themselves (K-college). The 30+ participants work and socialize together for 2 intensive weeks, forming collaborative teams that are often sustained electronically once they return to their home campuses.

In addition, another institute has been based on the CIWIC model.

—*ECAC in K-12* <http://www.hu.mtu.edu/ecac>—

For the last 5 years, under the direction of Dr. Dickie Selfe, an additional grant-supported summer workshop, Electronic Communication Across the Curriculum (ECAC), has been offered to Michigan's Upper Peninsula K-12 teachers and middle and high school students. The first week of the course is held at Michigan Technological University; the second week of the course is held virtually using Web-based technologies and tools.

The focus of ECAC is to explore the productive uses of communication technologies across the curriculum to improve the quality of writing, speaking, listening, designing, and so on, of students and to improve their attitudes toward the language arts in general. This professional development workshop is unique in that it is held in concert with a 1-week Student Technology and Leadership workshop filled with middle and high schoolers from the same institutions as the teachers. These students are encouraged to go back to their home institutions and provide support for teachers who are using communication technologies in their classes.

—The Importance of CIWIC and ECAC—

These workshops are compelling because they begin with the premise that pedagogical concerns should be considered first and that innovative technologies can best be integrated into teaching and learning activities after those concerns are addressed. They are also based on the assumption that innovative teachers are most productive when they can spend extended periods of time working on their own projects in the company of like-minded educators and support staff. The support staff need to be available as teachers identify learning objectives, learn new technologies, integrate those technologies into their classes, and then assess the effectiveness of their approach and redesign their techno-pedagogy for the next iteration.

—Sustaining these Workshops—

To develop this type of long-lived workshop, we have relied heavily on the intellectual vigor of the directors who not only conceived and direct the efforts, but promote it at the many conventions, presentations, and workshops they attend during the year. A core of visiting scholars and interdisciplinary faculty and graduate students in Michigan Tech's Rhetoric and Technical Communication Program are called on each year to add both theoretical and practical depth to the workshop. The CCLI facility, a student-run, and student-financed technology-rich facility receives financial support from CIWIC and ECAC and provides the physical and virtual workspace for participants during the month of June when these workshops are in full bloom.

Step #3: Operationalize instructional goals through technologies, environments, systems, and people. The third step of the process outlined in this chapter involves English and language arts teachers—cooperating with students, technical support staff, administrators, and other stakeholders on the design team—in operationalizing a list of instructional goals. In this stage, the design team builds on the instructional goals they have identified to articulate a set of operational goals—that is, increasingly concrete decisions about what should go on in computer-rich teaching and learning environments on a day-to-day basis, and how the material resources of such environments should be deployed to achieve a community's set of instructional goals.

To operationalize instructional goals, English and language arts teachers need to work with other members of a design team to consider how students' communications needs and faculty members' pedagogical concerns might shape the following areas in concrete ways:

- interfaces
  (physical and virtual)
- networks and systems
- technical support
- technology budgets
- professional development
- hardware and software

- access
  (faculty and student)
- maintenance
- furniture
- general ambience
- staffing
- scheduling (lab hours)

As an example of this process, consider the following list of operationalized goals for the CCLI (Fig. 3.3). These goals were derived directly from the instructional goals identified in Fig. 3.2.

To trace this process more specifically, consider Operational Goals #1, #3, and #7 (Fig. 3.3). All three of these *operational* goals—which focus on the day-to-day operation of the computer-supported facility—focus on creating an environment that allows for social understanding of composing tasks. These three operational goals are all derived from related instructional goals—Instructional Goals #3 and #4 (see Fig. 3.2), which articulate the faculty's general instructional commitment to helping students understand the social nature of composing/communication tasks.

Working from these operational goals, faculty members, students, and technical support staff in the CCLI decided to arrange the computers in pods as a method of supporting student-to-student exchanges, purchased a software package that allowed multiple collaborators to comment on shared papers, and set up a system of networked computers that would facilitate collaborative exchanges among individuals and groups who could not meet face to face. These same operational goals convinced the design team in the CCLI to establish online venues in which students could transfer documents from one computer system to another so that users could collaborate across platform boundaries, designate "Group" folders in which

OPERATIONAL GOALS

Goal #1 Purchase and maintain software and hardware that will support a socially situated, process-based approach to communication and the teaching of communication.

Goal #2 Provide CCLI access to any student enrolled in a communication-intensive class and to any instructor teaching such a class.

Goal #3 Make sure the CCLI is flexivle enough to support communication communities of all sizes: individuals, small groups, whole classes, etc.

Goal #4 Make sure the CCLI is administered on a policy level by a communication faculty member and staffed on a daily basis by consultants who have expertise both in communicating and the teaching of communication.

Goal #5 Provide hours that are flexible enough to accommodate individuals' communication habits and needs as well as groups' communication habits and needs.

Goal #6 Provide adequate technical support for maintianing, repairing, and modifying computer hardware and software so that communication faculty do not have to assume this role.

Goal #7 Ensure that CCLI policies encourage process-based communication, communication as thinking, and communication as social action.

Goal #8 Provide a budget administered by a communicaion faculty member and sufficient to support staffing, scheduling, software/hardware purchases, and technical support.

Figure 3.3 Operational Goals for Michigan Tech's CCLI.

class members could drop off and pick up documents, identify noncomputer areas in the CCLI where students and faculty could meet and talk about their composing efforts in face-to-face encounters, encourage eating and drinking in the facility as a way to support social exchanges that happened around collaborative composing tasks, and set hours of operation that allowed students to meet and discuss their composing efforts during and after normal class hours.

Step #4: Continue to build and change computer-rich environments from a position of strength. The process suggested in this chapter provides teachers of English and language arts with a strong foundation of core educational values and concrete operationalized articulations of these values that they can use to shape technology-rich teaching and learning environments. From these goals—both instructional and operational—a design team can construct arguments for financial resources, staff, space, curricular integration, technical support, professional development, and hardware and software that are based on educational expertise, student input, and technical expertise.

This stakeholder-centered design process can also help English and language arts teachers think through large-scale institutional initiatives that focus on technology in ways that are both careful and broadly informed. For instance, when administrators suggest a top–down technology initiative like outfitting campus labs with wireless computers, creating a laptop program that involves every department and student in a university, or putting all the courses in a particular department online, literacy professionals who have gone through a stakeholder-centered design process can use the instructional and operational goals they have derived—as well as the expertise of other stakeholders on their design team—to consider the initiative systematically and from a broader range of perspectives.

Armed with an informed sense of students' needs and teachers' instructional goals, for instance, design teams can argue that a focus on equipment *alone* cannot serve as the basis for a successful technology initiative and that a broad range of educational and material resources are required to support such initiatives: Additional professional development opportunities, technical support staff, open lab hours, and computer access for students are among only a few such resources.

Not all technology challenges facing a department or program are top–down nor are they focused on initiatives that involve brand-new technology efforts or learning environments. Many such challenges are ongoing, and many have a history. For instance, a design team may find themselves confronting the challenges attendant to a computer-supported teaching and learning environment that has existed for a number of years, but now needs upgrading, reinvigorating, or reconceiving. A team-driven, user-centered design process that is based on clearly articulated sets of instructional and operational goals can make this decision-making process more coherent as well.

Imagine this scenario: A school's central technology support people have a long-term relationship with a particular vendor. That vendor offers departments what appears to be some remarkable savings. They will replace all PCs in a teaching and learning environment with flat-screen workstations that include almost no moving parts at $200 per station (the "thin-client solution"). These stations—which cannot operate as stand-alone computers—are to be connected to powerful centralized servers. The vendor claims that standard office software will work seamlessly and quickly on these stations and reduce the cost of replacing an entire lab by two thirds.

Such an offer sounds intriguing on a financial level, but the perspective of different design-team members might find it less satisfactory. Certainly, in this case, English language arts teachers on the design team would want to look at the vendor's solution from the perspective of the core teaching values suggested by a list of instructional goals. For example, if these faculty are committed to the instructional goal of "helping students understand that composing, in many media, involves a complex recursive process of planning, drafting, revising, usability testing, refining, and editing," they may want the team to explore some probing instructional questions: How accessible will these new workstations be for students? Will the new workstations and system support processes of planning, drafting, and revising as successfully as the current system? Will the new system be available from off campus where an increasing number of students work? Will the new system support process-based composing approaches in multiple media (e.g., video projects, multimedia projects, design projects) that elementary, secondary, and college composition classes are assigning with increasing regularity?

The design team may also want to look systematically at the vendor's proposal from an operational viewpoint. For instance, if the design team is committed to the operational goal of "providing adequate technical support for maintaining, repairing, and modifying computer hardware/software/netware so that English studies or language arts teachers do not have to assume this role on their own," they may want to explore the impact of the new system on the technical support staff and their workload. How might such a system change the physical nature of a computer-rich facility or the virtual nature of an online environment? Will it be amenable to a stakeholder-centered approach to systems development (the users being teachers and students working in English or language arts programs)? The design team might also want to consider the proposal from the perspective of a technical expert who can corroborate the vendor's specific claims and seek the advice of technical experts at other institutions who have implemented these systems before. Other members of the design team, too, might contribute by examining the solution from their own perspective.[1]

The claims I make with this scenario are evident. First, the structure of a stakeholder-centered design team highly desirable because it provides English and language arts teachers the perspectives and commitment of multiple stakeholders who can help make a computer-supported teaching and leaning environment work productively and effectively from the perspectives of users and maintainers of the facility and systems. Second, the process of identifying core educational values and articulating them in instructional and operational goals—can help a design team formulate a much broader perspective on most technology initiatives and challenges and much more convincing arguments for specific technology-related solutions or initiatives. Such arguments are more convincing not only because they are based on well-documented professional evidence that can be gathered by English and language arts educators, but also because they will be based on the literacy needs of real students and on the expertise of technical support staff.

The process of developing instructional and operational goals based on students' literacy needs and core educational values is not painless. Indeed in some educational settings, it can be contentious. Yet these goals provide some basis for thinking carefully about technology within the

---

[1] By the way, many of the questions asked in the last several paragraphs can be answered in the affirmative. The thin-client solution may offer more access to technology off campus; it may reduce the maintenance load, and it is certainly cheaper than buying fully functional workstations throughout a lab/classroom. This means that new technologies just might improve our teaching and learning environments under certain conditions. What our goals provide us, once we decide to make changes in our facilities or systems, is a clear roadmap for assessing the change. If we initiated a "thin-client solution" because of cost, because it gives our students access to expensive software off campus, and because it reduces the maintenance load for technology professionals, we can assess those possibilities directly. We can also compare any improvements to changes in the other instructional and operational goals that will, undoubtedly, be influenced as well. We can then measure the answers to these questions: What do we gain? What do we lose? What are the relative merits of what is gained and lost?

frame of literacy instruction—and not simply from the perspective of bits and byte discussions, the cost of software and hardware, or even, sadly, the number of available electrical plugs on the wall of a computer lab.

One nice example of a department that put their pedagogical objectives up front before engaging in technological experimentation comes out of Penn State University. *(Dickie Selfe)*

Distance Education in the Department of English at Penn State

Stuart Selber
Department of English
Penn State University
University Park, PA 16802
selber@psu.edu

The Department of English at Penn State teaches courses over the Internet to a worldwide audience of motivated students. Our current efforts focus on service courses in business and technical communication and leverage the centralized resources of the World Campus, an outreach unit at Penn State that provides crucial pedagogical and technical support to academic departments.

We are engaged in distance education because our graduate program is committed to responsible instructional practices in the computer age. Which is to say that as humanists our efforts in this relatively new area are primarily energized by opportunities to revisit basic educational assumptions, test the social claims made about distance education, and prepare future teachers who can operate both effectively and judiciously in online environments. From our perspective, departments that foreground the values of English studies will find distance education to be a productive site for literacy education, one that can even influence the shape of resident instruction in positive ways.

The institutional culture at Penn State centrally contributes to our successes in distance education. In fact, we would discourage ambitious initiatives that are not adequately supported. Although English departments everywhere have been invited to move their courses online, it is important to wait until the conditions are right for you and your students, a maneuver that is essential to the establishment of truly sustainable activities. In our context, this meant holding out until we could implement a development process that recognizes—and rewards—the enormous amount of time and energy required to create valuable online

---

courses. What might such a process involve? For us, the decisive elements were significant release time for faculty and graduate students; organized tutorials in WebCT, the environment used at Penn State to deliver distance education; and assistance from the talented instructional and graphic designers who work for the World Campus. I should note that we funded our initial activities with seed monies that symbolize a serious commitment to our project at the highest levels of university administration.

If the institution contributes to our successes, so too does a departmental approach that deliberately integrates distance and resident instruction. Although the literature often characterizes online education as a radical enterprise, we have chosen to capitalize on—and reinforce—the strengths of our department, which include a strong doctoral program in rhetoric and composition and such nationally visible scholar-teachers as Cheryl Glenn, Jack Selzer, Keith Gilyard, Marie Secor, Elaine Richardson, Rich Doyle, and Don Bialostosky.

The result has been a progressive agenda for distance education that unites rather than fragments the department, clarifies instructional aims, and prepares graduate students for the 21st century in ways that are responsible and manageable. There are two focal points for our integration efforts. The first is graduate seminars in rhetoric that have been expanded to encompass the theoretical complications of literacy technologies; students in these courses consider computers through the lenses of various social theories. The second is a robust teaching practicum that prepares new writing teachers for instruction at Penn State. This practicum not only covers traditional pedagogical concerns, but also the thorny issues that arise when teaching with technology. Because our online classes mirror our on-site classes, all graduate students in rhetoric and composition have the opportunity to teach a distance education course before graduation.

In summary, our distance education efforts have been effective because we keep our professional values in mind as we author and teach courses; our institution appreciates and supports our endeavors; and we exploit the strengths of our department. These factors, in our view, are pivotal to the business of sustainable distance education in the humanities.

To learn more about distance education in the Department of English at Penn State, visit these Web sites:

The World Campus at Penn State
<http://www.worldcampus.psu.edu/pub/index.shtml>

English 202C, Effective Writing: Technical Writing
<https://courses.worldcampus.psu.edu/welcome/engl202c/>

A BRIEF CASE STUDY: VALUING COLLABORATION
THROUGH USER-CENTERED DESIGN

How does one go about creating the physical and virtual environments in which we and our students work? This chapter suggests employing a user-centered design team that begins by assembling a set of clearly articulated instructional and operational goals and then uses these goals to make decisions about a wide range of issues in a computer-supported teaching and learning environment. English and language arts teachers, among all stakeholders in such environments, should understand the importance of letting instructional goals—and operationalized forms of such goals—drive computer-based pedagogical efforts, drive the arguments they make when decisions about a new or redesigned facility are being made, and drive economic priorities.

It is often difficult, however, for English and language arts teachers to imagine how user-centered design teams—even when they are guided by instructional and operational goals—can actually shape, over time, the nature of technology-rich environments for teaching literacy. To these readers, discussions of instructional and operational goals may seem too generalized and, too abstract to help drive intricate and complex discussions about the architecture of online and onsite spaces, software and hardware purchases, human support systems, and budgeting decisions.

To help trace the processes of user-centered (or stakeholder-centered) design and identify the values of user-centered design teams more precisely for these teachers, we ask readers to consider a brief case study focused on an instructional goal that many English and language arts faculty consider central to their pedagogical approaches: "encouraging collaborative exchanges among teachers and students."

A design team might begin the process of operationalizing the goal of encouraging collaboration by focusing on the pedagogical implications of this complex term. English and language arts teachers may understand collaboration from one perspective, but other members of user-centered design team—students or technical support staff—might contribute additional understandings. A more robust definition of collaboration—informed by these multiple perspectives—could influence decision making on several levels.

One definition of collaboration, for instance, might center around students collaborating with each other on communication projects in and outside of class time. Designing a physical space around this understanding, it makes sense to arrange workstations in pods or small-group clusters that allow several people to work around one station. The physical space might also include rolling/swiveling chairs so people can easily turn and talk, monitors that move and flex in many ways or in ways that simply do not block collaboration, and lots of workspace around each workstation.

A design team may also decide, however, that students and teachers should be able to collaborate both on and off computers. In such a case, wireless laptop computers might help make classes more flexible when combined with rolling tables and chairs; arranging computers around the edge of the room with a large, central conference area might allow students and teachers to turn away from the computers and face each other more easily. In some situations, breakout rooms or spaces with networked computer projection could encourage the kinds of collaboration that some design team might feel essential to teacher and student constituencies. Clearly, definitions of collaboration—what is meant by that word and when it becomes an important aspect of instruction—can help determine design decisions about room size, furniture, computer foot prints, networking, lighting, sound, software, and projection capabilities, among others.

A user-centered design teams might also be assigned the task of operationalizing this goal—encouraging collaboration—in a virtual—or online— teaching and learning environment. Such environments generate an enormous number of options for collaboration. Shared network drives can be made available from local and remote sites. Modes of online synchronous and asynchronous communication obviously allow for valued kinds of collaborations as do visual conferencing systems (interactive TV and desktop conferencing systems). Of course all manner of electronic and print publishing can facilitate collaborations at many levels. Discussions about where and when students (and teachers) can get access to virtual teaching and learning environments will figure into the design team's work as well: Do teachers and students expect to work with each other, off-campus experts, and students from other labs or sites? Do they expect to access them from traditional classrooms, from home, from businesses, from public libraries, or from other schools? Most institutions are experimenting with distance education efforts that are either entirely online or available via interactive TV (ITV) systems. Some courses are hybrid combinations of face-to-face, online (usually using some Web-based system), and ITV events. Others are labeled *distributed learning courses* because they are for residential students, but do not meet in traditional classes (or meet less frequently) and are held primarily online from distributed locations either synchronously (in real time) or asynchronously.

All of these local efforts and resources need to be considered by a design team in operationalizing the goal of encouraging collaboration, and the differing perspectives and input of various team members will prove essential. A design team considering how to encourage collaboration in an ITV environment, for instance, may receive some bad news about the realities of their system, just as a local Michigan school district did when they investigated their ITV systems. They learned from experienced teachers that proctors at remote sites are not always available and that the additional planning time for teachers of these courses is both substantial and inconsistently rewarded by administrators. From technical support staff members, the team learned that audio and video quality often varies and is inconsistent; faculty are often required to run the system as they run their classes because administrators consider the expenses involved in hiring additional technical staff support to be prohibitive; and the equipment that drives such systems needs to be regularly updated at great expense. From student members, the design team learned that TV monitors are too small or too inconveniently located to make graphical displays visible, or that the tuition costs for such classes are often higher than those associated with conventional courses, and that class schedules varied from school to school and made attendance inconvenient or impossible—even for individuals who were interested (D. Holmier, personal correspondence, Phoenix Project, 2002).

CONCLUSION: RELY ON A STAKEHOLDER-CENTERED DESIGN PROCESS

How does one go about creating the physical and virtual environments in which we and our students work? This chapter suggests employing a stakeholder-centered design team that begins by assembling a set of clearly articulated instructional and operational goals and then uses these goals to make decisions about a wide range of issues in a computer-supported teaching and learning environment.

Literacy professionals, most among all stakeholders in such environments, should understand the importance of letting instructional goals—and operationalized forms of such goals—drive computer-based pedagogical efforts, drive the arguments they make when decisions about a new or redesigned facility are being made, and drive economic priorities. Although the design of computer-rich teaching and learning environments is necessarily a collaborative process, few other stakeholders will want or be able to contribute the professionally informed perspective of literacy teachers and scholars. English and language arts teachers, therefore, should be committed to taking on this role—bringing pedagogical concerns to the center of the design or redesign process of technology-rich environments.

Scott Sherrill is constantly planning new and reinvigorating established computing facilities in the Hancock, MI school system. In this very rural, financially challenged system, he is always being pulled many ways by involved stakeholders. Having a plan of action, however, has helped him justify the tough technology, policy, and human support decisions he has had to make. *(Dickie Selfe)*

Creating A Transparent Computer Lab

Scott Sherrill <scott@hancock.k12.mi.us>
Hancock Public Schools
Hancock, MI

In computerized instruction and in traditional instruction with technological components, the computer lab should be as easy to use as possible. In fact, its use should be transparent to the instructor and students. The equipment should be intuitive in use, readily accessible, and reliable. Listed below are several points to consider when planning and creating an instructional computer lab.

Consistent Hardware

This may seem like an obvious step toward creating a transparent computer lab, but often because of financial constraints, grants, and educational funding patterns, computer labs have mismatched hardware and peripherals. Consistent hardware makes support easier. There is a single set of drivers to download and support, a master image of what's on the hard drive of a typical machine can be created, and extra parts can be shelved to replace components as they fail. There should be special-purpose equipment and computers testing new software, but the special-purpose equipment should not be counted as a "seat" for group instruction.

Number of Seats

No matter how perfect the technical support team, computer hardware will fail at the worst time. When scheduling a lab for group use, always have at least 1-2 extra machines per 25 users expected to use the lab. If a computer fails before the group arrives or during the instruction, there will always be an open seat to accommodate the unforeseen.

Projection Equipment and Lab Layout

There are several different layouts that can be used in a computer lab. Each encourages or discourages collaboration or instruction in its own way. There are several great studies available on computer lab layout for further investigation. Pods may make collaboration easier; computers facing the wall may allow for quick surveillance and turning away from computers for discussions; rows focus students' attention toward one place in the room; etc.

It's important to have some mechanism to project the instructor's screen for student viewing. Projection can be done on the wall or on each individual station. Projection allows the student to compare their screen with the instructor's screen and stay with or catch up to the group.

Consistent Software

Nothing is more frustrating to an instructor than having some software missing or configured incorrectly. It's also important, especially to the technically uncomfortable, that the software be located in the same location on all lab machines. There are two main ways to achieve consistent software packages. The most popular is to clone a master copy to all the lab machines. The second method is the client/server method. The students use client machines as terminals to a more powerful server, which does the work and computation. In the client/server method, the client machine is simply a portal to the server. Current examples would be xterminals, Microsoft Terminal Services, and to some extent Macintosh Netboot.

It's also important to keep the images consistent once they have been created. Consistency can be kept through various hardware and software tools that prevent preferences from being saved or inadvertently changed [some recommended packages?].

Instructor's Responsibilities

It's important for the instructor using the lab to take some time and familiarize him or herself with the lab. Often software in a lab setting is installed differently than the instructor's personal or office computer. Instructors should also ensure the software is accurately installed by following handouts in the computer lab. By reviewing the handouts the instructor will know beforehand what screens look differently and what problems may be encountered.

Instructors should also have a backup plan. In case of a power outage or other major unforeseen problem, there should always be a backup plan to keep the group focused and working.

All students will work at a different pace if possible instructors should have some way to allow faster students to proceed ahead of the group and slower students to keep up.

Transparency

Transparent systems don't have to be totally invisible. Teachers and students should (if they want) be able to understand how their labs work and why they are set up the way they are. However, for day-to-day use, the class' attention should be focused on the educational tasks at hand, not the hardware, software, and room architecture.

Goal-driven design and development is just as important when developing entirely online systems. In this collaborative resource site, Bertram (Chip) Bruce has embedded his commitment to inquiry-based learning. As a result he not only makes resources available ,but also makes it possible to search, collect, and rearrange that material. He provides a space for teachers to talk to each other while they integrate these materials into classes across the curriculum. *(Dickie Selfe)*

The Inquiry Page: A Collaboratory for Curricular Innovation

Bertram (Chip) Bruce <chip@uiuc.edu>
University of Illinois at Urbana-Champaign
Champaign, IL 61820
<http://inquiry.uiuc.edu/>

The Inquiry Page is a Web site for collaborative curriculum development. It supports a range of activities in which educators are encouraged to investigate, create, discuss, and reflect. Teachers inquire through their access to resources on teaching and learning, including quotes about inquiry teaching, articles, project links, curriculum units, and content resources. They communicate with other teachers through various online communication media. They construct their own versions of curricula using an online inquiry unit generator. They express themselves through these units and through sharing both literal and textual photos of their classrooms.

Background

All learning begins with the learner. What children know and what they want to learn are not just constraints on what can be taught; they are the very foundation for learning. Dewey's description of the four primary interests of the learner are still appropriate starting points: inquiry, or investigation—the child's natural desire to learn; communication—the propensity to enter into social relationships; construction—the delight in creating things; and expression, or reflection—the desire to extract meaning from experience. Dewey saw these as the natural resources, the uninvested capital, "upon the exercise of which depends the active growth of the child."

But, as Dewey recognized, schooling is not just about the individual. It is the coming together of the child's interests with those of the society. The disciplines we study in school represent centuries of collective thought as well as the interests of the larger community in maintaining itself by communicating its knowledge and values to the next generation. The Inquiry Page <http://inquiry.uiuc.edu/> is about how teachers weave a learner's interests with those of society. It does this by supporting teachers as they share their successes and their collective expertise (Bruce & Davidson, 1996; Bruce & Easley, 2000). The page currently supports teachers and learners of all ages and curricular areas.

Inquiry Units

The Inquiry Page fosters the online creation of Inquiry Units by teachers (or students). Each unit starts with a guiding question and provides a space for activities of Investigation, Creation, Discussion, and Reflection. The user fills out a Web-based form that leads to an XML-formatted data structure. When the unit is called up again by the same or another user, a dynamic HTML file is generated. The latter can be used by students as they conduct their inquiry. In addition, students can edit a copy of the unit, thus using the curriculum Inquiry Unit as a place for their own work.

The cycle employed in the Inquiry Page unit generator presents an idealized model for inquiry, not to constrain our account of inquiry, but rather to serve as a reminder of the range of activities that might be involved. The danger in any description of a process is that the reader may infer that that description is the only or the ideal form of that process; or that the aspects of the process are steps to go through in some linear fashion. The intention here is not to specify the only or the ideal process. Nor is it to identify rigid steps to follow in doing inquiry. Instead, it is to present in an organized way some of the important aspects of inquiry that might be supported in a successful learning environment. Inquiry often leads to new ideas, results, theories, questions, etc. that can be communicated with others. This communication is central to the whole inquiry process, and our classroom environments ought to have a place for it.

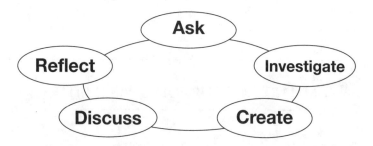

Figure 1. The inquiry cycle used to enter Inquiry Units.

Some Elements of the Inquiry Page

Quote of the Day: A collection of writings on teaching and learning, with a special emphasis on those that expand our conception of what learning can be.

Links to Resources: A dynamic incorporation (using Digital Windmill) of the Open Directory category: Reference: Education: Learning Theories: Inquiry Based Learning. This category is edited by the Inquiry Page development group.

Evaluating Inquiry Instruction: A web page linking to articles, presentations, and other resources regarding the special issues of evaluating inquiry-based learning.

Inquiry Units: A searchable data base of units for inquiry-based instruction across grade levels and subjects.

Inquiry Partners: A growing collection of partner projects, courses, and schools.

Conclusion

We welcome your feedback, your contributions of Inquiry Units, and your inquiries regarding participation in the Inquiry Page project. Please write to chip@uiuc.edu.

References

Bruce, B. C., & Easley, J. A., Jr. (2000). Emerging communities of practice: Collaboration and communication in action research. *Educational Action Research, 8*(2), 243-259.

Bruce, B. C., & Davidson, J. (1996). An inquiry model for literacy across the curriculum. *Journal of Curriculum Studies, 28*(3), 281-300.

Dewey, J. (1956). *The child and the curriculum & The school and society.* Chicago: University of Chicago Press. (Original works published 1902 and 1915).

A SUMMARY AND THE FOLLOWING CHAPTERS

This chapter suggests that we attend to students' literacy needs, formulate instructional goals from these needs, and then operationalize the goals in ways that make sense to a user-centered design team. By doing so, we put English studies and language arts professionals in a position to influence the design or redesign of both online and physical technology-rich environments in productive and effective ways.

Chapter 4 addresses two 800-pound gorillas that typically sit in the corner as we plan technology-rich environments:

1. The need for technology support so that teachers can learn and use these environments effectively.
2. The need for on-going financial support.

800-Pound Gorilla 1

It seems most difficult for English studies and language arts professionals to admit that we need ongoing, desk-side support to make our efforts sustainable (perhaps partly because of the fiscal restraints under which we work; see Gorilla 2). Without that support, our efforts to engage more than the estimated 5% to 10% of faculty who are considered early adopters in technology-rich instruction will be limited. Whether we accomplish this type of support face to face or at a distance or both, we are going to become (I would argue "should become") more dependent on student technology workers. My approach early in chapter 4 is to describe in more detail the specific benefits of putting students and student workers at the center of computer-supported teaching and learning environments. I provide examples of K–college institutions that have developed student support systems as a component of building their culture of support.

800 Lb. Gorilla 2

In a recent conference I suggested:

> We now find ourselves required to look up and stare with new eyes at the mundane: lighting, tables, chairs, the shape of rooms, the shape of online environments, wiring and wirelessness, hardware and software, and most importantly at the humans around us who make our cyborg lives possible.

The unstated assumption in that paragraph is that we all have the ability to do something about those mundane, but important, artifacts without considering first budgets and financial constraints. Instead I feel under the same spell that has entranced the rest of our related disciplines for so long: our ability to ignore financial issues—the one thing that makes our consideration of that list possible. I approach this topic by suggesting some of the benefits of a stakeholder-centered design process on budgeting matters. Of course, money plays an important role in the learning, teaching, design, and collaboration that goes on in and around computer-supported teaching and learning environments regardless of whether our colleagues want to attend to financial matters. The final sections of chapter 4, then, includes several budgeting models that seem to offer (alone or in combination) English studies and language arts teacher leaders some promise for increasing the longevity of technology-rich instructional systems.

Strangely, even in this information and digital age, we rarely ask training teachers or teachers new to technology, K–college, to imagine themselves debating and leading discussions about support systems or budgets. The following chapter should help illustrate to these colleagues how important it is to engage in discussions of this type and to provide small steps toward a vision that will help them productively influence their current technology-rich instructional environments.

4

MAKING SYSTEMS WORK IN SUSTAINABLE WAYS

STUDENT TECHNOLOGY ASSISTANTS AND EFFECTIVE FISCAL MODELS

SUMMARY OF TOPICS

▶ Two 800-Pound Gorillas (p. 85)
▶ Student Workers at the Center of Things (p. 86)
  • An Argument for Including Students (p. 87)
  • A Case Study (p. 87)
  • More Arguments for Involving Students (p. 90)
  • Creating Student Technology Assistant Programs (p. 92)
  • Talking to Teachers with Experience (p. 97)
▶ Creating a Sustainable Budget and Fiscal System (p. 105)
  • The Entrepreneurial Model (p. 111)
  • The Grant Funding Model (p. 115)
  • The Student Lab Fee Model (p. 117)
  • The Central Computer Funding Model (p. 118)

When English language arts teachers discuss the pedagogical issues associated with technology-rich environments, they frequently fail to recognize that both the issues and environments are intimately bound up with two important and related concerns: the ability of technical support people to keep up with the demand for their services and the ability of the fiscal resources to provide material support for humanities-based computing. These issues lurk in the corners of our major decision-making efforts like two 800-pound gorillas, unacknowledged but impossible to completely ignore (for most of us). This chapter suggests that we must face these concerns early and frequently.

In most educational computing environments, the options for support—both human and financial—are already constrained. As a greater
percentage of colleagues have begun to demand rapidly changing technologies, these constraints have reached the crisis stage at many institutions.
Even well-healed institutions are finding it difficult to hire and retain
enough competent and imaginative support people—especially when
these same individuals can command salaries in the private sector that far
exceed those of the teachers and scholars they serve in the academic
realm. The current fiscal climate in most academic institutions is also constraining. As technological solutions become more sophisticated and complex, many institutions are discovering the need to fund the costs of additional electronic and digital infrastructure, additional support personnel to
maintain this infrastructure, and additional professional development for
existing staff members.

Within such crisis contexts, most English/language programs find
themselves at a distinct disadvantage. Seldom funded adequately; often at
a loss for adequate sources of grant funding; and frequently plagued by
dwindling budgets, salary compression, the ever-increasing cost of supplies
and services, most departments find themselves exceedingly hard pressed
to muster the additional costs associated with technology-rich teaching and
learning environments.

Given this reality, I would suggest that—for many programs and
departments—the crisis surrounding support is both real and dangerously
close. In this chapter, I suggest two strategies for dealing with this situation.
The first strategy involves reassessing our technological relationship to the
students with whom we work every day. The second strategy involves
understanding and identifying the right institutional funding models that
can, in combination, help fund sustainable technology-rich environments.

STUDENT WORKERS
AT THE CENTER OF THINGS

In most institutions that have managed to sustain a technology-rich teaching and learning environment for use by English and language arts teachers, you will find at least one person who will argue that students have a
substantial role to play in the design and support of technology-rich communication environments. Many teachers and administrators, however,
have legitimate concerns about placing responsibility for technological sup-

port—at any level—in the hands of students. In response, this section begins with some arguments and justifications for involving students that readers might want to consider within the context of their own institutions. As you might have guessed, from my perspective, goal setting plays a role.

AN ARGUMENT FOR INVOLVING STUDENTS

This book has outlined a processes-based approach to establishing sustainable, computer-rich communication environments in a way that avoids the dynamic of blame and helps build a culture of support. The goal, of course, is to sustain, over time, innovative and appropriate instruction in English and the language arts. Such a system is almost impossible to set in motion, however, without involving students.

In the technology survey described in the Preface, the effort of recruiting, supporting, and deploying a corps of student technology assistants (STAs) was often cited as a key element of successful programs and acknowledged as one of the most effective solutions to the support crisis documented by the American Association of Higher Education publications (Gilbert, 1997). At the end of this chapter, readers will find a list of K–12 professionals responsible for the integration of WWW technologies in their schools who are willing to serve as a contact person for people interested in establishing such programs.

Yet it is clear from talking to English studies and language arts professionals that the task of creating and maintaining student technology assistant (STA) programs also requires a sustained effort. It will happen over time and only if it is built into the instructional and operational goals constantly being defined and refined by interested stakeholders.

A CASE STUDY: FROM GOALS TO SUSTAINABLE STUDENT-CENTERED TECHNOLOGY ENVIRONMENTS

To understand the concept of weaving a theme of student support into the goals of a computer-rich environment, it may help to consider a short case study. Look again at the list of instructional goals for the Center for Computer-Assisted Instruction (CCLI) in the Humanities Department at

Michigan Technological University (Fig. 3.2). The final goal in that list is stated as follows: To encourage communicators to learn and share successful communication strategies. Although this goal does not explicitly mention computers or other communication technologies, it does have a clear technological corollary: Within an increasingly technological culture, individuals must understand how to learn and share effective strategies in computer-rich communication environments.

In the CCLI, both the original goal and its technological corollary provide the intellectual rationale for involving students in all aspects of planning and operations, teaching and learning. The communication skills, value, and attitudes that students practice in these contexts—in and around computer systems—are essential to their success as individuals living in an increasingly complex technological culture. The value of these communicative practices and attitudes—and of this learning environment—cannot be underestimated for students.

As Margaret Mead suggested in *Culture and Commitment*, adult English teachers may not be able to teach students all the skills and values they need in an increasingly technological culture—primarily because contexts are changing so fast that adults have limited personal experience in such environments. Students, often have to assume a major portion of the responsibility for teaching themselves about new forms of communication; to do so, they need to locate environments in which they can experiment with the new literacy practices that surround technology—communicating in and through multimedia texts; writing for gaming and simulation environments; and exchanging information in MOOs, MUDs, and other digital environments.

In an environment like the CCLI, student technology consultants end up teaching themselves much of what they learn. Moreover, they must often direct their own learning—to a great extent—as they fulfill their responsibility for mentoring new consultants and designing new network interfaces, managing and directing large-scale technological projects, or assisting a teacher in a single computer-supported class. They often find themselves teaching small groups of peers to use digital technologies and writing documentation for a new piece of software. These situations offer a second-level curriculum for our majors, who are primarily technical communicators. The ability to teach themselves, mentor others, and teach in small groups are essential workplace skills. It is hard to imagine a professional occupation that does not require the same of its employees. What happens in a technology-rich environment supports Brown and Duguid's contention that some of the best learning and work occurs when teachers are not around and when the formal trappings of a classroom and curriculum are absent. In such environments, students learn to learn from each other and learn to direct much of their own instruction.

Recognizing the value of this student-centered learning environment—and the importance of the instructional goals that helped shape such an environment—faculty, staff, and students working in the CCLI have also identified several operational goals that shape this computer-rich learning space in ways that are open to student involvement. Those goals include the following:

- ▶ Work to ensure that the CCLI is flexible enough to support communication communities of all sizes: individuals, small groups, whole classes, and so on.
- ▶ Make sure the CCLI is administered on a policy level by a communication faculty member and staffed on a daily basis by student consultants who have expertise in both communicating and teaching of communication.
- ▶ Provide hours that are flexible enough to accommodate individuals' communication habits and needs as well as groups' communication habits and needs.

In the landscape bounded by these goals, CCLI student consultants (a mixture of engineering, humanities, technical communication, and other majors) provide support and instruction for communities of individuals, small groups, and entire classes. Without their presence and expertise, these communities would suffer and in many cases would never exist at all. Student consultants also provide expert guidance in technical matters and help other students develop rhetorically effective media projects: from traditional essays to Web pages, from multimedia texts to digital movies, from new media poetry to new media scholarship. These students come from a variety of disciplines, but they often seek out more formal instruction in computer-based communication classes given their personal interests in digital environments. They are also familiar with the digital literacy skills, approaches, and attitudes of the next generation of digital communicators.

Perhaps what is most impressive about the student consultants in the CCLI is the fact that most of these student consultants volunteer their services—they are not paid. Their own personal investment in this learning and teaching environment is certainly secured by the 24/7 access they have to the labs. Yet they are also attracted by the range and scope of their involvement in making important decisions, the skills and values they can learn in this space, the esteem in which they are held by teachers and other students who depend on them, and the satisfaction they get from teaching themselves and others. These consultants support online systems, research new products and systems, and make most of the technology purchases. They train new consultants, address user suggestions, assist teachers, maintain equipment, and provide enough staffed hours so that individual's and groups of students can complete their work with knowledgeable coworkers around them. They serve as psychologists, cheerleaders, and experts.

Periodically, administrators or staff members from other areas of Michigan Tech question the value of maintaining a computer-supported teaching and learning environment that depends so centrally on student consultants. Often these questions arise when people observe the significant amount of time and effort that goes into recruiting and maintaining the corps of CCLI consultants. Such challenges often begin with valid concerns: Many students do lack administrative and teaching experience and personal maturity when they begin in the CCLI, and a good team of student consultants does require the supervision and attention of talented teachers who could be occupied with other much-needed assignments. Moreover, good student consultants develop over time, and it is difficult to maintain a consistent level of expertise when a quarter or more of the consultants graduate or go on internship assignments each year.

The best answer to such challenges, however, are the instructional and operational goals (mentioned earlier)—they make sense to faculty and academic administrators and can be translated into language that makes sense to technicians and IT professionals as well. They are the foundation of what makes the CCLI work for student technology workers and faculty.

MORE ARGUMENTS
FOR INVOLVING STUDENTS

There are additional reasons, other logics, as well, that will help convince stakeholders that student-based, technology-assistant (STA) programs are worth the effort and cost. Among them is the significant matter of money. Except in the extraordinary cases of institutions enjoying great wealth and resources, it is unlikely that K–college institutions will be able to find the kind of human instructional and technical support necessary for sustainable programs without taping the interest and ability of our student bodies. Most teaching institutions simply cannot afford to hire credentialed professionals in the numbers necessary to maintain an ambitious technological agenda. The experience of many professionals who have been working in the instructional technology arena for some time now—among them Steve Gilbert and Cynthia Selfe—confirms that at most institutions students are already involved in some aspect of designing, running, or assisting in the digital environments they and their teachers inhabit.

In an ideal educational world, this would not necessarily be the case. Funding for education would provide the professional desk-side support that teachers and students need to learn and make productive use of new technologies. On-site technical support people, instructional and interface designers, programmers, content experts, learning theorists, and assessment specialists would all be available at appropriate moments as literacy professionals prepare dynamic, innovative, technology-rich instructional experiences. Most of us, however, simply do not live in such a world. Instead the programs and departments within which such teachers work face increasing technological and instructional responsibilities and are armed with shrinking budgets. As a profession, we do not have the financial resources to hire professionals to do this work on the scale our curricula and pedagogies demand.

For many reasons, this is a blessing. When students are involved in the design and operation of technology-rich teaching and learning environments—at all levels—faculty can directly observe the practical benefits of such theoretical concepts as participatory design, "learner-centered" curricula, cross-age tutoring, self-sponsored learning, project-based instruction, and process-based pedagogy. Through an involvement with technology-assistant programs like the one we have described at Michigan Tech, literacy professionals get to see students teaching themselves and benefiting from real-world instructional experiences. Teachers also get to see students developing the new-media communication skills and values that will serve them well in an increasingly technological world, and they get to learn from students about the power of these new literacies in their lives.

One final bit of logic that supports the effort to establish and sustain a corps of talented STAs comes out of the marketplace. Most sectors of the economy—technology and information services, banking and finance, health and medicine, education and social services—and many professional-level jobs are now calling for entry-level employees who can both learn new communication technologies appropriate to their fields and make use of the new media that are changing the way people work alone and in concert. Students who have served as technology assistants are uniquely prepared for such tasks, and—for this reason—they often find themselves in great demand on graduation. English studies and language arts programs that have some interest in making sure that their graduates are recruited and employed may find STA programs to be an effective tool in this effort.

There are, of course, challenges that accompany STA programs. Faculty working with such programs, for instance, are not generally interacting with students in conventional courses. Thus, they may have difficulty securing teaching, service, or research credit for their work. This is especially true when groups of student technology assistants are interdisciplinary, when they involve students enrolled in a broad range of programs and majors. For this reason, programs that incorporate STA programs should make sure to identify such work as part of the credit load borne by faculty and staff members involved in technology projects. These challenges, however, are minor when compared with the benefits that STA programs yield, and educational professionals lucky enough to work with successful programs will find the effort enormously productive and rewarding.

CREATING STUDENT TECHNOLOGY ASSISTANT (STA) PROGRAMS

The real question, then, is not "Do we need student support?", but "How do we go about continuously recruiting, educating and involving talented young people to take up support positions?" Further, we must ask, "How do we make sure that both parties benefit from the partnership?"

The stakeholder-centered design process described in chapter 3 can provide an answer to both questions. Such an approach serves to recruit students because it involves them in shaping the technology-rich environments at important levels and in ways that affect their lives and values, their identities and sense of confidence, their future, and the new-media communication practices that will characterize this future.[1] English and language arts teachers already know that young people hunger for opportunities that challenge them, that are productive, and that make a difference to those around them. What we are just beginning to understand, how-ever, is that faculty who work with sustainable and well–run technology-rich environments—whether online or in physical facilities—can offer

---

[1] For an example of the training that our volunteer student consultants receive, see http://www.hu.mtu.edu/ccli. Look under CIT (consultants in training) for materials and policies we have collected over the years.

these opportunities to students. Such facilities allow faculty to place the right students in the right situations—over and over again. Given the importance of STA programs, then, training and recruiting a student support staff should occupy at least as much planning time as the time spent on physical and virtual architectures. The following sections provide five different strategies for involving students in technology-rich teaching and learning environments.

Strategy 1: Recruit Students Out of Every Class Taught and Ask Colleagues to do the Same

The most effective strategy for recruiting STAs can be enacted in the classes that English and language arts faculty teach. Teachers know the students well, have often seen them react to technology-rich activities, have observed their "people" skills first hand, and have some experience working with them in collaborative situations. Teachers who already use computer technologies in their classes can be encouraged to pass along the names of the students who have the potential to develop into talented technology assistants. English and language arts teachers are often good scouts for such individuals because they also realize that the best STAs are often not technology know-it-alls, but people who have a gift for communicating, an interest in new technologies, and a talent for working with others, including teachers.

Many STAs are recruited through personal contact—invitations extended by a teacher staff member who can describe the benefits of supporting technology-rich teaching and learning environments. Such invitations frequently offer students an acknowledgment of their talents and a boost in their confidence. Also effective for recruiting STAs are face-to-face visits to classes. During these visits, teachers and experienced STAs can describe the value that student workers can add to instruction at an institution *and* the benefits that the students receive from the experience. At MTU we mention these benefits:

- technology training that emphasizes the person and project, not just the technology,
- pay (if salaries are available),
- experience that will be of value in applications and job searches,
- letters of recommendation to accompany applications,
- access to advanced technologies that are difficult for individuals to purchase and maintain,

▸ academic credit (through official classes, internships, or independent study), and
▸ promotion to more prestigious, exciting, or advanced positions
in the program or at the institution.

English and language arts teachers should also consider recruiting
STAs from programs that employ student helpers in other parts of the university: writing centers, libraries, central computing groups, computer science or computer engineering departments, teaching effectiveness and
faculty development institutes, and other departments who are well funded or have goals that focus on effective communication.

Strategy 2: Allow Student Workers to Assume as Much Control and Responsibility as They Can Handle

Most people do not join groups and organizations unless they feel empow-
ered or engaged by that group. Students feel the same way. The student
technology consultants in the CCLI, for instance, have always been willing
to take on substantial responsibilities when they realize that they will also
have a real say in how those systems and facilities are run and configured,
how policies are made and procedures established, and how budgets are
spent and hardware purchased. Experienced consultants work with a budget of approximately $140,000 each year that comes from student lab fees.
Yet even institutions without direct access to lab fees can make budgetary
decisions accessible to STAs, inviting them to voice opinions about technology use, policy, and purchases within a program or department.

STAs also enjoy taking on other responsibilities that make a difference
to users: among them, designing and implementing workshops for faculty
and students; mentoring other students or new technology assistants; and
designing policies for security, access, and resources. STAs can also assume
the responsibility involved in advanced technology support positions
(which are often well paid by student standards), maintenance of software
installations, system administration, and programming of online systems
like educational MOOs.

All of these approaches for involving students as technology assistants
encourage them to recognize a personal investment, a stake, in the future
of the technology-rich instruction in their English studies or language arts
program.

Strategy 3: Use the Attraction of Technology to Encourage the Formation of Student Communities

Young people are highly attuned to the social organizations—both formal and informal—around them. Many students who perceive their postmodern lives as fragmented and unconnected seek community in stable groups or organizations that offer them positive and productive outlets for their talents. The time they spend with other students and professionals helping support technology-rich environments can offer such community experiences. In the CCLI, for instance, there are always several groups of students who combine their social needs with an interest in technology support. Our online and onsite facilities provide them with a valuable point of contact—a reason to form supportive technological and social communities.

Unfortunately, college and K–12 institutions do not always place such community-building activities high on their list of priorities. In most institutions, however, drop-in computer facilities can be designed to serve as a nexus for community formation—as long as teachers, programs, and departments designate them as spaces in which students can and are supposed to meet and interact around language tasks. Often students who are provided with even minimal requirements for community formation—a safe and comfortable place to work and interact with others—will begin the process of learning and teaching on their own as they provide both technical and social support for each other. They get to know each other, learn who to work with and who to avoid. They form social groups, game together, eat out, play sports, and flirt. In short, they form communities.

Strategy 4: Support Student Technology Assistants— and the Formation of Student Communities— in a Variety of Ways

STAs will do a great deal of recruiting on behalf of computer-supported teaching and learning environments that value their involvement. Literacy professionals who want to encourage this process, however, might want to consider the following suggestions:

▶ provide STAs a space within which they can make decisions (e.g., arrangement of furniture, purchase of hardware and software, rules for eating and drinking, design of interfaces);

- ▸ provide STAs some organizational status (e.g., titles, opportunity to make decisions, chance to teach other students or teachers);
- ▸ provide STAs access to special online work/play spaces or work-stations;
- ▸ design communication systems around the ways students and STAs interact (e.g., instant messaging, e-mail, Web chat, and face-to-face exchanges);
- ▸ provide STAs an opportunity to follow their academic interests (e.g., involving computer science majors in programming projects, asking design majors to help create Web sites; involving business majors in budgetary oversight projects).

In short, literacy professionals need to think about how to provide students with a reason to care about the technology-rich environments in their programs and departments. If students are allowed to help design and maintain these spaces, they have a reason to invest in the success of computer-supported teaching and learning environments.

Strategy 5: Develop Institution-Wide Programs That Pay Students for the Work They Contribute

Many programs and departments that enjoy a sustainable, computer-based environment for teaching and learning have identified ways to pay (or repay) students for the work they contribute in classrooms, teachers' offices, labs, centers, and online environments. Often this pay takes the form of curricular credit, on-the-job experience related to students' majors, hourly wages (often through work-study programs), prerequisites (e.g., access to technology, recommendations from teachers, satisfying social involvement), or combinations of these rewards. In return, students attend training sessions and take on tasks within the department or around the institution. In many of these programs, students support teachers who want to learn new technologies; integrate technologies into a course; teach in a lab, classroom, or online environment; or assess and redesign the computer-based strategies being used. They conduct initial technical troubleshooting, media support, applications instruction, and many other useful services.

In institution-wide programs that extend beyond the bounds of an English studies or language arts department, talented students may also find themselves working in specialized labs, learning and writing centers, open-access labs, online help centers, and faculty development centers. Sometimes their training takes place in courses built into various curricula. In other cases, they are treated more like professional staff members whose training takes place in conjunction with their job outside formal academic curricula.

TALKING TO TEACHERS
WITH EXPERIENCE: STA PROGRAMS

STA programs can be small or large, confined to a single English/language arts program, or extended across an entire school—all depending on local needs and resources.

Many K–12 teachers who use technology in their classes, for instance, start informally, collaborating with their own students, their own children, or even their children's friends. As they grow confident, these teachers often begin helping their colleagues and make a serious contribution to the *appropriate* integration of technologies on an individual class level. Nancy Patterson, for instance, now a faculty member at Wayne State University, served as a teacher at Portland Middle School in Michigan when she wrote the following description of a relatively informal program of student technology assistants:

> I've had . . . success . . . using student mentors in classrooms where the teacher is not . . . computer literate. . . .

> A teacher might want to have students use presentational software, but the teacher doesn't know anything about how to use that kind of software. So, I . . . gather a group of . . . students, arrange with their other teachers for them to miss class, and then ask them to help the students in the other class. I'll help the teacher decide what the expectations should be, and show the teacher a bit of how the program works so he/she can be competent enough to start the students out. I generally arrange for anywhere between 3 and 7 kids, depending on the size of the class that will be in the lab. "My" kids station themselves around the lab and work one-on-one with the students after the teacher has gone through the initial start up ritual. My kids bail their peers out of any technical jams they get into, and they show them short cuts, etc. That frees the teacher . . . to answer curricular . . . questions.

Earlier this year, I had students help out in a special ed. classroom that had read a Gary Paulsen novel. The teacher and I worked up a web hunt using Filamentality, a website that allows teachers to create web searches. The teacher and I set up the web search, and posed the questions. My students then helped the special ed. kids get on the internet, etc. It worked great. It always works great. And it allows kids who aren't necessarily academic stars to strut their stuff.

. . . [I]t isn't anything systematic. I go to work when a teacher comes to me. But more and more of our teachers now know how to use the lab, and most of our kids know more than the teachers. So the need for peer mentors diminishes each year. . . . [But] we will be installing a new lab this fall, so the mentors may go . . . full tilt again. (personal correspondence, January 2001)

An example of a much more formal STA program in a public school setting comes out of Baltimore City College, which despite its name is an inner-city public high school. STAs in this setting become members of a technical support team and take a specific course in which they receive training. In this course, students complete part of the 75 hours of service work Maryland requires for graduation from high school. Liz Dunbar, Technology Coordinator in this setting, explains the program in these words:

Tech support to the whole school is a significant part of my Advanced Technology Systems course. This is an 11th and 12th grade elective, with a prerequisite grade of 85+ in the introductory course and approval of the teacher (me). The students repair, expand, cajole, support, train, etc. technology and users throughout the school. . . . Doing my job as Technology Coordinator would be either impossible or impossibly costly without the help of these kids.

The official web site for the program (< http://baltimorecitycollege. org/faculty/techdept/tekcours.htm >) adds the following information:[2]

---

[2]For a review of the comprehensive approach taken by this inner-city high school to deal with the social and technical issues that swirl around technology use in the public schools, see their Web site: www.secondwindgh.org/advtech/. You can also contact Liz Dunbar, the Technology Coordinator, teacher, and Webmaster responsible for most of these initiatives: Elizabeth Dunbar < secondwindgh@comcast.net >

This elective for upper level students focuses on operating systems, network fundamentals, introduction to C/C + +, website development and management, animation, and onsite help desk for computers and users school-wide. The Advanced Tech Student Tech Support Team plays a major role in the design, building, management, and maintenance of City's computer and network operations.

A more complete and candid discussion of this program—in question–answer format—in provided in the following *Sustainable Practice*.

Student Technology Assistance Programs have enormous potential for helping alleviate the support crisis faced by most K-12 educational institutions. But resistance to these programs often comes from the technology coordinators themselves. Those in the districts I've worked with are so pressed for time (many also teach and have other administrative responsibilities) that they see this effort (training student technology support personnel) simply as more work. They also are the first to hear about abuses committed by students using their systems and so feel under pressure to keep access contained. Their e-mail inboxes are rarely filled with the productive success stories that their systems help make possible. Liz Dunbar, thankfully, provides an example of a high school program that is both academically challenging and technologically productive. *(Dickie Selfe)*

A High School Student Technology Assistant Program out of Baltimore City College HS

Liz Dunbar <edunbar@greenmount.org>
http://baltimorecitycollege.org/advtech
http://baltimorecitycollege.org/faculty/techdept/tekcours.htm

A 39-year veteran teacher nearing retirement but "still having fun," Liz Dunbar has built a technology support system at Baltimore City College (a high school, not a college) using the technical literacy talents of students (10th-12th graders) and a technology curriculum with these characteristics: highly constructivist, student-centered, project-based, and problem-solving. The content of the courses include "operating systems, network design, intranet and Internet operations, animation, website development and management, and the management and maintenance of City's school-wide network" (http://BaltimoreCity College.org/advtech/). Lest people think that only technology-trained teachers can take on this sort of program, consider this. "I've been at City College since 1978 and have taught-instrumental music, Latin, Man and His Culture (multidisciplinary social studies course), English I - American Lit, English III - American Life in Literature teamed with US History, College Writing, Creative Writing, and Yearbook (15 years)." Other institutions interested in developing curricula like City College's should look for teachers with the technological interest and drive when they are trying to build such programs. As Ms. Dunbar suggests, find somebody who is "easily bored."

The advanced technology course is part of a Technology Program offered at the school. Courses include

Introduction to Technology Systems

The course brings students to levels of competence in academic computing modeled on the Microsoft Office User Specialist Program.

Information Technology in a Global Society

This elective course in City's International Baccalaureate Diploma Program looks in depth at the components of computing to explore social implications and ethical considerations of technology in today's world.

Advanced Technology Systems [The course most relevant here.]

This elective for upper level students focuses on operating systems, network fundamentals, introduction to C/C++, Web site development and management, animation, and onsite help desk for computers and users school wide. The Advanced Tech Student Tech Support Team plays a major role in the design, building, management, and mainte-nance of City's computer and network operations.

Introduction to Computer Programming in Java

This elective for upper level students introduces the concepts and methodologies of computer programming from an object-oriented approach. (See <http://baltimorecitycollege.org/faculty/techdept/tek cours.htm> for more on each course.)

The Logistics of the Course and Support Team:
(The following is excerpted from e-mail conversations held on 19, Jan. 2001 and 07, Aug. 2001.)

Tech support is an integral part of my Adv Tech class, which meets daily from 11:35-1:05. They do their tech support during the class period. If a teacher requesting help can't work with that time frame (but 99% do), the help request moves up the ladder to when I can get to it to do it myself—which is usually a significant delay, another reason they let the kids in. Since there is a lunch period scheduled during the first half of my class and also after it, occasionally I will let kids go to lunch during my class so they can work in a teacher's room during what normally would have been their lunch period. Since the work/class period is midday we have few interruptions for activities, which we handle the same way we handle absences—if you're not here, you can't do any tech work that day. There'll be more work tomorrow, and if you keep missing work eventually your grade suffers and you don't get the service hours you need to graduate. (Maryland requires 75 hours for a high school diploma.)

At the beginning of each class, I ask for status reports on yesterday's work, report feedback from teachers they've worked with, and reel off work requests I've received since yesterday; I also outline the academic work for the next few days. The students each decide which work orders they want to tackle, how much time they want to spend on tech support, and how much on the academic work that day. All the academic work is online and so can be self-scheduled, acknowledging deadlines. Then I write passes for those who need to work elsewhere in the building, and everybody gets to work based on their individual choices for the day. Adult time required is about the same as teaching any other class—lots of prep time and lots of monitoring and helping out as needed. At the end of each class, students write a daily log, which is turned in and graded weekly, and they also record all tech work in a general tech support log so that everybody (including me) can see the status of work orders (and so I can keep track of tech support service hours).

It's a semester class, so each semester I start with a new batch of 20-25 kids. Enrollment [in ATS] is by word of mouth, self-selection but with permission of the instructor. I give permission to kids who I know by reputation are self-starters or who convince me they are, kids I've taught in other classes and know their style, kids who aren't scared away by my questions, or 10th, 11th, and 12th graders who really want the course and can justify any Intro. to Technological Systems grade below 90; I turn away very few, I scare away a few more.

Background and Administrative Support

The program got started 3 years ago because the administration wanted a technology elective to make the senior year program more rigorous. It continues to be strongly supported by the administration—not only because it is a rigorous course, but because it saves the school a *lot* of money in technology support.

For example, the school system last winter received a donation of thousands of Pentiums from a government agency; they are still in storage awaiting funding for upgrading and installation—but we're picking up our 155 next week because the Adv Tech class will upgrade and install them for our school. We'll have to buy some parts and more software licenses, but the cost will be trivial compared to that of new computers.

The course also fits into the school's college preparatory magnet public high school curriculum in several ways:

1) It meets the state technology credit requirement for graduation (for students who, for whatever reason, don't take the Introductory to Technology Systems course);
2) It provides an advanced tech course for students who are not in the Advanced Studies program (who take "Information Technology in a Global Society" <http://baltimorecitycollege.org/ib /itgs.htm>);
3) It expands the relatively short list of available electives in our rigorous college prep. curriculum;
4) It provides another way for students to fulfill the Maryland requirement of 75 hours of service work for a high school diploma.

A Final Word

"The reality is that to make any kind of program work takes energy and vision." (Liz Dunbar, Technology Coordinator . . . Webmaster . . . System Administrator . . . Teacher, personal correspondence, Mon, 16 Sept. 2002.)

Colleges and universities also find it useful to establish institution-wide STA programs. Interest in these programs is perhaps demonstrated best by the frequency of presentations on the subject on the Teaching, Learning, Technology Group's Webcast interview site (http://www.tltgroup.org/, "Webcast Interviews"). In the winter and spring of 2002, three different online interviews were conducted at this site:

February 5, 2002: "Student Technology Assistant (STA +)
    Programs: Addressing the Support Service Crisis"

Robert Harris, Assistant Director of Instructional Technology,
    William Paterson University < http://www.wpunj.edu/stc > ;

Lisa Star, Director of Instructional Technologies, South Dakota
    State University < http://learn.sdstate.edu/star/stf.htm > ;
    and

Paul Fisher, Associate Director, Teaching, Learning, and
    Technology Center, Seton Hall University < http://tltc.shu.
    edu/ace/index.html >

April 9, 2002: "Student Technology Assistant Programs"

Paul Bowers, Director of Teaching and Learning with
    Technology, Buena Vista University
    < http://tltc.bvu.edu/default.asp >

Linda J. Eddy, User Support Services Manager, Johnson C.
    Smith University

Joe Douglas, University of Milwaukee-Wisconsin
    < http://www.uwm. edu/IMT/STS/HR/ >

May 14, 2002: "Assessment of STA Programs"

Lisa Star and Dr. Allan Jones, South Dakota State University
    (see above)

Steve Ehrmann, The TLT Group < http://www.tltgroup.org/ >

The STA program at William Paterson University—a midsize, 4-year,
institution enrolling approximately 10,000 students and one of nine state
colleges in New Jersey—was one of the first college-wide efforts in existence. This effort (< http://www.wpunj.edu/stc >) provides an interesting
example at the collegiate level because it was not mandated or funded by
the state—as is the case for the STA program at South Dakota State
University—nor is it associated with a wealthy institution that can support
other large-scale technology initiatives, like Seton Hall University. Robert
Harris, the Director of this STA program, notes:

> WPUNJ is anything but a rich school—the fact is that we are very
> poor, in a relative sense. That is what makes this kind of program so
> very important, and that is just how the idea arose; the use of students

as colleagues became imperative exactly *because* we could not afford to hire professionals! (personal correspondence, August 7, 2002)

The essential components of William Paterson's STA program are fairly easy to describe, but of course they require remarkable dedication and skill to implement.[3] The program is directed by a full-time professional—Robert Harris, < harrisr@wpunj.edu > —but run, to a great extent, by students with seniority in the program. A pyramid system of student-supported training (4-day workshops twice a year and ongoing education throughout the year) keeps the pipeline full of interested and energetic consultants. Students are paid on a sliding scale from $8 to $10 per hour and limited to 10 to 20 hours of work a week. Students in the WPUNJ program pick up points for completing tests and projects as they go. Their duties range widely depending on the IT needs of the institution. In July 2002, for instance, WPU had seven different teams of consultants working on different projects (< http://www.wpunj.edu/stc >). These students collaborate closely with faculty, staff, and students and accumulate a remarkable portfolio of skills, approaches, and attitudes.

One of the best ways to convince college or university administrators of the value of STA programs is to grow them locally. Joe Essid, the Writing Center Director at the University of Richmond, for example, developed a training course for STAs that fits into the English composition curriculum and the university's writing-across-the-curriculum program (< http://writing.richmond.edu/training >).

The Humanities Department at Michigan Technological University has developed an informal STA program based on those students working in the Center for Computer-Assisted Language Instruction. This program matches interested teachers with student consultants recruited from Humanities classes. These STAs work to provide teachers with access to hardware and software, expertise, and the support they need to encourage productive technology-rich instruction.

Two-year institutions also create and sustain STA programs. Often these programs face special challenges because students have little time for training and there is a high turnover rate. Pamela Ecker (< PamEcker@aol.com >), for example, describes the STA program at Cincinnati State Technical and Community College:

---

[3]My comments here are based on three sources: the Web site listed in the text, discussions with the Student Technology Consultant (STC) director, Robert Harris, and a short precis he wrote back in the summer of 1999 justifying a fee increase that would support the STC program < http://www.wpunj.edu/stc/precis > .

> Most lab techs [student workers] have taken classes in the lab before they start work. . . . Successful completion of Intro to Mac or an equivalent Windows course is a requirement for getting the job. . . . [Students] participate in "running the lab" via occasional meetings with the Supervisor. Student lab techs are paid. [Technical Communication] students who work in the lab also can earn co-op credit (Co-op credits are required in the degree program). Working in the lab is considered a good "first co-op" so students who work there are relatively inexperienced, but . . . not computer novices. Ongoing training is not provided so many lab techs cannot support all users of all tools. The Writing Center goals emphasize providing support to the novice lab users. (Survey response, D. Selfe, 1998)

All of these STA programs recognize that students will continue to learn, adapt to, and integrate new communication technologies into their literacy profiles much more quickly than adult educators. STAs can help literacy professionals who are trying to develop a cutting-edge multimedia program or provide a basic computer-support program for novice users. The experiences of teachers mentioned in this chapter suggests that both informal and formal STA programs can and probably should become a valued part of educational landscapes in most schools. Teachers can look forward to establishing and interacting with STA programs because they attract talented, motivated students. Administrators and institutions can appreciate the more mundane fiscal reasons for implementing STA programs. If interested stakeholders can be convinced of the value that STA programs will bring to teachers, classes, and overworked technical support personnel, then budget-conscious administrators can start negotiating local constraints and begin building the culture of support at their institution from the students on up.

CREATING A SUSTAINABLE BUDGET AND FISCAL SYSTEM

The first chapter of this book suggests an important sequence of priorities for teachers of English and language arts interested in establishing a sustainable program of computer support: people first, pedagogy second, and technology (and technological concerns) third. As Sean Williams notes, however, the real material concerns of paying for technology must occupy teachers and administrators at some point in the process of planning:

> Computer Classrooms (CCs) [and I would suggest that the same holds true for online environments as well] have been an important part of writing instruction since the mid 1980s, yet little scholarship concerns the roles that directors of computer classrooms play in maintaining these facilities. Based on a review of scholarship of CC administration and an informal survey of CC administrators, this article argues that CC directors walk a tightrope between the role of teacher and manager and that we need to focus on building partnerships to maintain our facilities, because we simply cannot do by ourselves everything that his complex role requires of us. (Williams, 2002, p. 339)

In short, pedagogical needs must be balanced with technology concerns, including fiscal realities. Without pedagogical goals, English and language arts teachers will have no idea which technologies they need, and without attention to budgets, they will not be able to determine which pedagogical ambitions can be met and sustained effectively. "If you can't pay," Kate Coffield and her colleagues point out, "you can't play" (Coffield et al., p. 290). No other component of technology-rich environments influences instructional and operational goals more directly or broadly.

However, the specifics of who pays for the play varies greatly from institution to institution and is often invisible to most stakeholders. One of the findings of the 1998 survey mentioned in the Preface to this book was that stakeholders at institutions of higher education knew less about budgets than any other issue associated with their technology efforts. Yet the pressure to understand and deal productively with fiscal matters is building at educational institutions. Thus, until English and language arts professionals learn how to address the complex financial demands of technology integration, they will find it difficult to be entirely successful in the design of sustainable technology-rich environments.

Although it is difficult to compare the fiscal procedures for two institutions or even two projects, most technology-rich environments in English studies and language arts programs can be represented on a continuum of financial control. On one end of this continuum is local control. Departments with programs or computer-supported facilities on this end of the continuum—for instance, the Humanities Department's Center for Computer-Assisted Language Instruction (CCLI) at Michigan Tech—have local control over their entire technology budget, although they must operate within guidelines mandated by the institution. Thus, every single piece of hardware and software purchased and every person supported with a salary in the CCLI must be accounted for in a public budget, all of these expenditures are determined by the faculty and students working in the facility. (Appendix 4.1 provides a budgetary breakdown for the CCLI at MTU.)

On the other end of the continuum are computer-supported environments financed through a system of centralized control. At this end of the continuum, almost all budgetary items are considered to be part of the purchasing responsibility of a central IT authority—often one that remains unseen or unknown to English studies and language arts professionals.

Both situations can be a blessing and a curse. For instance, because the CCLI operates under a system of local control, students are provided the rare opportunity to help spend and balance our budget. Thus, they are involved in fiscal decisions that affect all aspects of teaching and learning environments—both online or in the physical facility. They can decide to allow students to eat and drink in the facility (and to replace the few pieces of equipment that are damaged over the years); and they can decide to purchase an experimental piece of hardware or software (and not to purchase something else); they can decide to raise the salary of an employee within a certain range (although they might have to reduce the number of employees they hire overall). The process of managing this locally controlled budget, however, is clearly awash in detail and difficult choices. Staff, faculty, and students have to attend to technological decisions that most stakeholders at other institutions can delegate or ignore all together.

In contrast, a centrally managed budget is often out of sight and out of the control of teachers, students, and even local IT professionals. Institutions and programs operating at this end of the continuum depend on a staff—usually consisting of IT professionals hired by the institution and working through a central office. This staff takes care of detail work without bothering literacy professionals or students with decisions about mundane matters.

In either situation, however, faculty can find it extremely useful to predict how much an online or onsite facility will cost—especially as they face a decision of establishing lab fees, preparing grants, interacting with central technology departments, or designing and proposing new digital teaching and learning environments. Not only are initial costs important to estimate, but amortized or replacement costs for these environments must also be considered in developing sustainable technology-rich instructional systems.

Although the majority of the 191 respondents to the 1998 survey knew relatively little about the budgetary processes that administrators used to support the computer-rich facilities in which they worked, some could provide very broad estimates of the categories of expenditures within their facilities, (see Table 5.1).

TABLE 5.1 General Categories of Budgetary Expenditures as Estimated by Workers in Computer-Rich English and Language Arts Facilities (Selfe, 1998)

BUDGET CATEGORIES	PERCENTAGE OF BUDGETS EXPENDED
Hardware	36%
Software	13%
Salaries and wages	43%
Expendables	8%

These figures are descriptive—insofar as respondents' estimates are accurate—of computer-rich facilities that generally take the form of labs or computer classrooms. Teaching and learning environments that exist entirely online—if they are not inextricably connected to physical facilities—may have a different fiscal profile. The hardware, software, and expendable categories for these environments, for example, may be significantly reduced because they exist entirely on networked servers, are supported centrally by institutions, and delivered to students via home or dorm computers. However, the percentage of salaries and wages in such online environments may increase because they depend on employees with specialized skills.

For some institutions, online teaching and learning environments work effectively to support teaching and learning. Depending on how such environments are planned and implemented, however, they can change the relationship among teachers, students, and technology. Online teaching and learning environments like WebCT or Blackboard, for instance, may serve not to reduce the overall institutional need for technology or students' need for access to this technology, but rather to increase it. Indeed the dynamic of blame is likely to be lively if students perceive the message from an institution to be, "We have provided teachers with the tools to create online classes and the network space on which to hold these classes. Now you must identify and provide your own workstations in order to access these classes." Unless institutions also provide students access to online classes through open labs or laptop initiatives, those individuals with the fewest financial resources will, as usual, suffer the most.

It may be useful to make some observations about the general patterns of budgetary expenditure for computer-supported teaching and learning environments. First, English and language arts teachers may rightly find it odd—even dismaying—that expenditures for hardware and software comprise only a slightly larger proportion of the budget than do expenditures for salaries of support staff. This is true even though most teachers and administrators who work with technology are well aware of the acute need for more support personnel. Raising the awareness of this issue is one role that teachers of English studies and language arts can play at an institution. Indeed the current lack of discussion about the human effort required to support computer-supported teaching and learning environments may be a contributing cause of the current "support crisis" that Steve Gilbert of the AAHE has popularized through his many presentations since 1997 (Gilbert, 1997).

A second observation has to do with the interrelatedness of the budget categories represented in Table 5.1. The category of software, for example, seems to represent a relatively small percentage of the budget, but software concerns have a substantial influence on how functional, valuable, and usable technology-rich environments may become to teachers and students. Hence, the importance of software as a factor in such environments may not be measured accurately or fully in budgetary terms alone. It is also difficult to estimate the expenditures associated with the installation of software, the effort of troubleshooting problems with software products, and the education students and teachers need to use software effectively. When these costs are factored in, the percentage of budgets associated with software may become much greater.

A third observation is that general budgetary breakdowns may provide little locally useful information. More useful may be budgets broken down precisely and amortized over an appropriate time period. The process of amortization is fairly simple. Staff, faculty, and students first determine what items go into the budget. Then each budget line—except salaries, wages, and expendables— are assigned an expected lifespan as indicated in the budget. For instance, in the Center for Computer-Supported Language Instruction at MTU—computer workstations are assigned a lifespan of 3 years, servers are assigned a lifespan of 5 years, furniture is assigned a lifespan of 7 years, and carpeting is assigned a lifespan of 10 years.

When all items are accounted for under such an amortized system, faculty, staff, and students can identify how much money they need to collect—from granting agencies, lab fees, institutional funds—each year to pay for each category of expenditure over time. Thus, if a workstation costs $2,000, the amortized cost of that workstation will run $666 a year for 3 years. At $5,000, carpet over 10 years will run $500 each year.

All amortized budget items are calculated and then added to yearly expenditures for salaries, wages, and expendables so that teachers, staff, and students can derive an annual budget. Such a system makes most financial decisions painfully obvious. For instance, if the staff, faculty, and students want to install additional servers, raise salaries, add storage space, provide special ADA-approved tables for students with disabilities, or purchase more software, they must adjust our amortized budget in other ways—making the carpet last another year, limping along on a slow server, and hoping that workstations will last for 4 years instead of 3.

At many institutions, the responsibility for various technology expenditures is divided among several units. In such a situation, departmental budgets, central university budgets, and IT budgets are tapped for different needs. Knowing who controls those budgets, how they are managed, and when the budgetary priorities are being determined are enormously important to literacy professionals who hope to create a sustainable computer-rich environment.

Whether budgets are locally or centrally located, united under one group or divided among several, it is crucial for stakeholders to understand and be able to talk about the specifics of long-term fiscal support for technology. Yet knowing what the budget *should* contain is not the same as locating sustainable funding—even though amortized budgets may help administrators argue for funding.

The following sections describe three models of sustainable fiscal support—beginning with the rarest, the entrepreneurial model, and working toward the more common, centralized funding. I provide a brief review of the advantages and disadvantages of each.

THE ENTREPRENEURIAL MODEL

The entrepreneurial model of sustainable fiscal support taps skills and attitudes that may seem foreign to many English and language arts teachers. Fundamental to this approach is the ability for a group of faculty to think of the literacy skills and abilities that they teach as marketable commodities. Web authoring, for example, is one of the most recent literacy skills in demand. Project management skills are also at a premium in this sort of fiscal system.

Teachers and students who choose this model realize that the activities on which they focus in academic courses—often, but not always, courses in technical communication and multimedia design—are likely to be valuable to community organizations, businesses, corporations, and governmental agencies. They must also be willing to market those skills and abilities continually to clients in the community and to attend carefully to the needs and expectations of those clients. Finally, student/faculty teams must be able and willing to produce materials that are useful and valued by clients both inside and outside academic institutions.

Most teaching and learning environments that depend on the entrepreneurial model use a team process. Within a team, some members have the responsibility of contacting clients—in industry, academic, or community organizations—and of convincing them to contract for products: for example, custom documentation, Web sites, user testing efforts, workshops, or research support. The other members of the team assume the responsibility of creating and delivering such products. The income from these efforts is generally used to purchase technology for use by the team—and often other students and teachers as well—and, in some cases, to pay team members for their efforts.

Several components must be in place for such a system to work well. If students are given academic credit for such work, the courses being offered must attract individuals who are both interested and capable of participating in a business venture. Further, the products marketed out of such courses need to be attractive to the clients paying for them. English studies and language arts programs that invest in such a model must value real-world communication efforts. In other words, there has to be a good fit between the expectations of faculty, students, and the curriculum before an entrepreneurial effort can begin or be sustained.

Although examples of entrepreneurial models of fiscal support are hard to come by, they are increasingly attractive to universities, colleges, and K–12 schools whose budgets are shrinking—even as the technological expectations of the general public are rising. Entrepreneurial projects tend to be headed by interested and talented faculty or staff—or teams of faculty and staff—who are responsible for technology-rich labs, classrooms, or online environments. One such faculty member is Dr. Sean Williams, who teaches in the Professional Communication program at Clemson University. This program, located in the Department of English, offers a

Master of Arts degree[5] and relies on a computer-supported environment called the Multimedia Authoring, Teaching, and Research Facility (MATRF). The MATRF supports the unique needs of the students in the Professional Communication program, and Williams works to provide state-of-the-art media development tools for this program.

To accomplish this task, Williams recruits masters-level students from the Professional Communication program who are interested and willing to work on Web development and information design projects with clients from local businesses and other academic units within the university.

The entrepreneurial model works well for Williams, the Department of English, and the Professional Communication students because it meshes well with so many components of the local environment: with Clemson University's tenure expectations, with Williams' talents and expertise, with the professional expectations of students in the program, and with the curriculum of that same program. Williams, for example, makes a habit of conducting scholarly research that bears on his team's entrepreneurial projects. He publishes frequently in the areas of project management, workplace literacy, and design of online systems. Students on Williams' team expect to graduate and find jobs within corporate or independent entrepreneurial positions that demand expertise in digital communication. These students not only need to develop their own expertise, but they also need to assemble professional quality portfolios for interviews when they graduate. The curriculum of the Professional Communication provides courses in areas of multimedia development, visual literacy, usability testing, and workplace literacy, among others—all courses with a heavy emphasis on communication projects and the rhetorical contexts within which they exist. In addition, at the departmental and university levels, Williams is encouraged to make community contacts and use the resources of this land-grant institution to help both business and not-for-profit institutions in the State of South Carolina.

A similar entrepreneurial effort has been set up at James Madison University and is detailed in the following *Sustainable Practice*. In this case, students who serve on entrepreneurial teams are also paid salaries. The remainder of the income from design projects goes into supporting technology and recruiting more clients with online or Web-related projects.

---

[5]The Clemson English Department is also designing both an undergraduate and Ph.D. program in professional communication. Both degrees will also depend on the MATRF or similar facilities and increase the need for expanded, sustainable financial resources.

Partnering with on-campus and off campus organizations can involve students and teachers in well supported technology-rich projects. Elizabeth Pass provides an example of how James Madison University's ITSC program has set up an entrepreneurial student technology assistant program that is both integrated into the curriculum and financially sustainable. *(Dickie Selfe)*

Technology-Rich Ties at The Institute of Technical and Scientific Communication at James Madison University

Dr. Elizabeth Pass <passer@jmu.edu>

The Institute of Technical and Scientific Communication (ITSC) at James Madison University is a stand-alone program within the College of Arts and Letters. Because we are a stand-alone program, we believe we are able to focus better on collaborating with other departments and university organizations, as well as with businesses and industry. We have been able to attain our goals of providing the bridge between academe and industry, successfully transition our students into the marketplace, and continue our professional development through these fruitful ties.

The Student Publications Group (TSC 490) is sometimes the genesis for many of our projects. However, various professors in the Institute generate interdisciplinary projects as they occur through interaction with individuals from other departments, programs, and industry. Often these projects are directed to the Students Publications Group or its Coordinator at the time. Some of these projects are used for internships and practicums, too.

ITSC – CIT Partnership

One of our "best" technology-rich efforts is our work with our university's Center for Instructional Technology (CIT). CIT has many programmers and graphic designers; however, just like many industry and business organizations, they need good technical communicators. We want our students to learn from them, and they in turn learn from us. So we have developed a partnership. We have a part-time student position reserved for the ITSC in the CIT. They have many projects from faculty all over the university who need documentation and technical communication expertise. They also work with us to set up internships in the CIT to work on these projects. These projects are large in scale and in many cases the projects will be used across the nation, not just at the university. We may have one student on a particular project, or if the project is large in scope, our Student Publications Group (a group of selected ITSC majors who work on print and online documents for 2 semesters'/6 hours course credit) will work on the project as a team. The following are a couple of the current projects that our ITSC – CIT partnership has yielded.

Virtual Pavlov2000 Software Documentation

The Virtual Pavlov2000 project is for a professor in the Department of Psychology. This application will allow students to simulate classical conditioning experiments, and it will contain over 60 minutes of live video. The CIT is developing the Macromedia Director 8.0 application that is designed for high school science students. The CD-ROM will be inclusive, and the ITSC's part is creating the online help files to go with the program. There is also the possibility of a teacher's manual, at a later date. We have currently had 2 of our students work successively on this project, using RoboHELP. This is a win-win situation: CIT has access to good technical communicators, and staff are collaborating with good writers; ITSC is able to place its majors in part-time jobs and internships where they are utilizing their technical communication skills while at the same time being able to work with specialized Web designers and computer programmers.

Digital Image Database

This database originated from the School of Art and Art History, but the General Education program and other universities are also using it. The Digital Image Database is a website containing a discipline-specific search engine that allows instructors to create their own slide shows based on their own criteria. The multimedia database contains approximately 65,000 thumbnail images of art and culture including sculptures, paintings, architecture, landscapes, furniture, drawings, maps, textiles, musicals instruments, photography, and jewelry representing Europe, Asia, Africa, South Pacific, and the Americas. By each thumbnail there is a complete description of the piece; these descriptions can also be annotated by each instructor's creation of a new class database. ITSC's role is to create the print and online help for the students and instructors, not only for James Madison University but also for the other universities who are interested in this database. This provides good experience for our Students Publications Group to work on a project for a large, public end user group.

This partnership with ITSC and CIT is providing TSC students valuable industry experience that they would not be getting in an internship or part-time or summer job for a few reasons: first, the students are getting to follow the entire project cycle; second, the students are watching a realistic, collaborative team work a project through to the product; third; the students are working on many different projects that utilize a variety of skills; and finally, the students are working on projects that are designed not for hypothetical end users but for real end users. These reasons add up to the ITSC – CIT partnership as one of our "best" technology-rich efforts here at ITSC, and one we hope that will continue to grow.

THE GRANT FUNDING MODEL

Departments or schools that choose to fund computer-rich teaching and learning environments through grant-writing efforts often find that the demands of a sustained program of grant writing parallel, in many ways, those of entrepreneurial efforts.

Fundamental to this approach is the ability of English studies and language arts teams to think of digital literacy skills, approaches, and attitudes in terms of the initiatives identified by specific granting agencies and programs. Teachers, staff, and students who can envision how their pedagogical efforts might fit with a range of such initiatives are likely to experience the most success with internal, state, and federal grants. Successful grant writing requires that teachers and staff imagine or sell the activities they would like to accomplish in their classes—placing these in the context of problems articulated by the granting entities. Project management skills are also at a premium in this fiscal model.

In the chapter "Surveying the Electronic Landscape: A Guide to Forming a Supportive Teaching Community" in *The Online Writing Classroom* (2000), some colleagues and I have outlined many of the approaches and resources literacy professionals might need as they take on grant writing efforts.[6] I would add here only two cautions. First, grant support for technology-rich environments requires continuous and wide-ranging efforts. The effort of writing grants, delivering what is promised in a grant application, and maintaining and tracking a large-scale grant project is considerable and requires a great deal of commitment. Hence, the rewards must be worth the effort. Small grants, for instance, unless they require a minimum of paperwork are not always worth the effort necessary to pull them off. In addition, maintaining the first grant for a computer-supported teaching and learning facility is only the beginning. Teachers, staff, and students will also need to think well into the future, usually years ahead, to research, write, consult, revise, and apply for subsequent grants.

During the last decade and for the foreseeable future, grant support for digital learning environments seems a promising source of funding. However, digital environments cost more in terms of technical and human infrastructure than can usually be financed through any one grant, even large ones. Grant opportunities tend to be focused around specific projects, and, by necessity, those curricular projects take up a great deal of time, leaving the teaching professional less time to focus on the day-to-day needs of the digital environment. At Michigan Tech, for instance, one effort of the Center for Computer-Assisted Language Instruction (CCLI) has resulted in a grant—secured in collaboration with the Delta Schoolcraft Intermediate School District—for an annual 2-week workshop on Electronic Communication Across the Curriculum (ECAC) designed for K–12 educators (< http://www.hu.mtu.edu/ecac >). This workshop is held on an annual basis and provides salaries to pay for some technical support people. These people, however, are primarily engaged in the ECAC project and are generally not available to help students and faculty users at large. The grant also pays for some lab maintenance and equipment (e.g., disk storage, an additional server, a projector). Without an already established computer-supported facility and additional ongoing funding for that facility, however, this grant would be insufficient to provide the online and physical facilities required to fulfill the 2-week obligations.

---

[6]In a section of that chapter called Financing the Exploration (pp. 290-292), we outline an approach similar to the one suggested in this book: create plan and vision by thinking about goals first, justify your plan in pedagogical terms, then look for funding from many sources. Readers of this book might find Appendixes A, B, and C of that chapter (pp. 310-315) quite useful. They include a list of categorized goals for teaching with technology (A), a description of what an amortized budget might contain (B), and a list of online and print-based grant materials (C).

At the same time, the ECAC project is one that should be pursued. It represents intellectually productive relationships between K-12 and university partners. It is exciting, valuable, and stimulating for the undergraduate and graduate students, many of whom plan to become educators. The ECAC project is also exceedingly satisfying and challenging for the faculty and staff members who work on it. In this sense, the project is well worth the effort expended on the grant that funds it. Moreover, this project repays the CCLI, the Department of Humanities, and Michigan Technological University handsomely with the good will of educators in the surrounding region. Alone, however, this grant project (or even a dozen like it) could not provide a sustainable budget for the CCLI as an educational facility.

THE STUDENT LAB FEE MODEL

Another common model for funding computer-supported teaching and learning environments involves the collection and use of student lab fees. Often such fees are instituted by individual departments or facilities that must find their own source of funding for technology. The motivation for charging such fees varies, but it is generally based on this economic philosophy: "Let those who use the technology pay for it."

At Michigan Technological University, for example, the student lab fees charged for disciplinary facilities cover the purchase of servers, the salaries for technology support staff, the furniture that students use, the cost of network ports, and even the card-activated security system on the doors. Increases in the student lab fee must be previewed by students who use the lab and reviewed by a campus-wide oversight committee. Because these fees are so important to sustaining technology within the Humanities Department, that unit makes sure that it has representatives on the university committee that review such fees. In addition, the department makes sure that faculty members serve on most ad hoc committees that shape the university's campus-wide technology policies.

Both advantages and disadvantages characterize the student lab fees model. If such fees are locally controlled and reviewed by a team of faculty, staff, and students, everyone receives quite an education in connection with budgets, the funding of upgrades, the cost of change, and the trade-offs inherent in making decisions about hardware, software, netware, human resources, and the physical infrastructure of an environment. Often in such democratized settings, public fora are held to inform student and faculty users about the lab fee income and facility budgets. A university committee may also be involved in this process and may need a separate presentation. Considering the pressure to find money for computing resources for groups other than students, this practice is a sound one—student lab fees should be audited by a university to ensure that they are spent in ways that directly improve the educational environment for students and not other constituencies.

Those programs and departments interested in establishing such a funding model might find it useful to read the Student Lab Fee section of Michigan Tech's Computer Advisory Committee document at < http:// www.hu.mtu.edu/CAC/1995 > .

THE CENTRAL COMPUTER FUNDING MODEL

The most conventional form of financial support for instructional computing environments comes from a central funding process—most often a computing fee applied to all students as part of tuition or in addition to tuition, and collected and distributed through the general fund of an institution. This process is not only difficult for faculty in one department or school to influence, but it may also make computer fees difficult to trace and secure for a particular computer-supported environment.

This model of central funding is also common in K–12 institutions. One result (probably indicative) was that, in a recent workshop for teachers in the rural districts of Upper Michigan, none of the participants knew when requests for computer equipment had to be submitted to the central district office. When the workshop designers asked the district's technology coordinators for this information, they learned that requests were due during the hectic final days of the school year in May (which had just passed). The teachers wisely began the process of building requests for services and equipment into their activities planned for the following year.

With a central funding model, much of the planning and operational work is removed from the shoulders of literacy professionals. Instead staff members in a central computing office institution take on these responsibilities. In addition, there is little duplication of effort in the technology research and purchasing process. One can take advantage of economies of scale, and students can often apply technology purchases to their student loans and grants. If centrally funded systems result in fewer responsibilities for faculty and cheaper prices, they often make it difficult to identify who within an institution is making decisions that affect a program's or department's technology efforts. Moreover, such a system may make it difficult for English and language arts teachers to understand the conditions under which these decisions are made, identify the assumptions that inform them, and learn about the timing of these decisions. In such situations, it may also prove difficult for faculty to identify all of the turf issues, personalities, and politics—departmental, school-wide, and even state-wide—associated with technological decision making

CONCLUSION

Paying close attention to budgeting processes in computer-rich teaching and learning environments is a valuable process for all stakeholders. Faculty and staff members who attend to such matters learn a great deal about the real costs associated with communication technologies—both human and financial. For some lucky students (graduate and undergraduate), the opportunity to become involved in making decisions about technology issues can engender not only a sense of ownership and commitment to technology-rich teaching and learning environments, but also an important intellectual habit of technological activism. This type of activism may be the best reason to establish a stakeholder-centered design process. If students develop sound intellectual habits of mind, when they graduate they can apply them to technology initiatives in local school systems, community programs, and workplaces in ways that make such environments more effective for the people who inhabit them.

As this chapter suggests, attending carefully to areas such as budgeting processes and STA programs is important to sustaining appropriate technology-rich environments. The attention paid to these areas can also help establish a culture of support that provides us with a venue for sustained agency.

The process of planning and designing truly sustainable computer-rich environments, however, also requires an ongoing effort of assessment—one that provides faculty, students, and staff dependable and systematic information about what works well and what needs to be improved. The final chapter of this books outlines an assessment process that:

▸ invites interested stakeholders to participate in an ongoing process of design,

▸ involves stakeholders without overburdening them, and

▸ allows stakeholders operating in unique institutional contexts to modify this process to fit their own needs.

5

ASSESSING
AND REDESIGNING
SUSTAINABLE
COMPUTER EFFORTS

SUMMARY OF TOPICS

▶ Three Assumptions about Assessment (p. 123)
▶ A Model of Assessment and Redesign (p. 124)
  ▶ Step 1: Identifying stakeholders (p. 126)
  ▶ Step 2: Defining issues and areas of interest on which
         to focus (p. 132)
  ▶ Step 3: Observing current sites of effort and involve-
         ment (p. 133)
  ▶ Step 4: Identifying possible sites for increased involv-
         ment and investment (p. 137)
  ▶ Step 5: Pinpointing and fine-tuning involvement
         (p. 141)
▶ Why Such a Complex Effort? (p. 146)
▶ Afterword: Final Summary and Comments (p. 149)

Because the work of creating and re-creating technology-rich environments for teaching and learning English and language arts is never really
completed, this chapter offers an ongoing process for assessing and

improving these spaces—spaces that teachers of English and language arts can help sustain over time. This process focuses on continual, *formative* efforts to shape computer-supported environments, not a *summative* end product—a yearly report or a faculty presentation that reveals only snapshot in time.

The team-based process of assessment and redesign suggested in this chapter helps stakeholders pay close attention to the social, pedagogical, technical, fiscal, and institutional components of digital environments, and to make sure successful practices and values are sustained over time by teachers, students, administrators, and staff members. The process also focuses assessment broadly on the needs of students, teachers, and other team members; subscribes to the concept of using assessment information proactively to conserve the ideals and pedagogies in which teachers believe deeply; and relies on the fact that English and language arts faculty can help manage, shape, and direct technological change that improves teaching and learning. This book and chapter are an unapologetic attempt to implement for our disciplines what Andrew Feenberg has called for in many publications on critical approaches to technology: an attempt to democratize the process of technology development.

One might reasonably wonder, at this point, what I mean by "technology." What technological development can literacy professionals hope to influence? As my friend and good colleague, Johndan Johnson-Eilola, has suggested, English studies, technical communication specialists, and language arts professionals no longer have the luxury of attending to any one technology. The systems we depend on (the cyborg entities that I have described earlier that combine social and technical components) are so closely associated with the literacy practices that we hope to instill in our students (see chap. 1) and so integral to our own instructional and intellectual work that those systems have become the technology that we must assess. For the purposes of this chapter and book, the designing and redesigning that we contribute to include instructional design (the choreography of teachers, students, and technology), lab design, interface and information design, the design of institutional relationships, fiscal relationships, among others. Indeed (paraphrasing Johnson-Eilola) the new media environments we now live in/with are so much a part of our lives that they constitute a "complex technical ecology," all of which we must attend to if we hope to have some control over our working, teaching, learning, and administrative lives (J. Johnson-Eilola, personal correspondence, April 2003). The short hand I use in the chapter then equates this complex technical ecology with the word *technology*.

THREE ASSUMPTIONS ABOUT ASSESSMENT

The process-based model of formative assessment outlined in this chapter is based on a set of three key assumptions.

First, no assessment project—suggested by this book—can succeed unless there are individual English or language arts teachers willing to commit time and energy to the ongoing efforts of observation, analysis, and change that should form the basis for all assessment efforts.

Second, assessment is a team sport. So the individual teachers responsible for *starting* an effort of ongoing, formative assessment must commit to seeking out and teaming up with other stakeholders who also have an interest in the continual improvement of technology-rich environments: students, technical staff members, information specialists, local and upper administrators, and other interested people from the community including parents, school district personnel, and corporate representatives. As this book argues, successful technology-rich environments—sustainable cyborg systems—depend on inclusive and ongoing processes of decision making by a team of stakeholders, each member of whom may be invisible from one perspective or another, or at one moment in time, but who collectively comprise the human heart of a cyborg system.

Finally, and perhaps most important, the processes of assessment should be closely connected to the processes of *user-based design and redesign* (what I also refer to as stakeholder-based design)—the continual process of attending to the needs and visions of stakeholders in shaping computer-rich teaching and learning environments. For this reason, I refer to the model described in this chapter as involving both *assessment and redesign*. The goal is to trace a specific part of this relationship to illustrate how inclusive processes of assessment can lead English and language arts teachers toward informed efforts of user-based redesign.[1]

Throughout this chapter, the term *assessment team* is used as a convenient term to refer to the group of stakeholders—English studies and language arts teachers, students, and other interested—who lead the

---

[1]In previous chapters, I alternated between the terms user-centered design and stakeholder-centered design. But in this chapter, to avoid unnecessary confusion, I opted to take up the single phrase, user-centered. The term user, then, refers to all stakeholders. These groups all "use" our physical facilities and online systems in their own ways. By definition, stakeholders have a stake in a technology-rich environments. That stake determines, to a large extent, their "use" of the environment.

assessment processes forward. Given the intimate and recursive relationship between processes of assessment and processes of user-centered
design advocated by this book, however, this team could just as easily consider itself a *design* group.

A MODEL OF ASSESSMENT AND REDESIGN

Models of assessment are often difficult to understand in the abstract. With
this in mind, this chapter uses, as an illustration, a case study of the assessment undertaken in the Center for Computer-Assisted Instruction (CCLI) in
the Humanities Department at Michigan Technological University. The use
of this extended case study is not meant to suggest that one set of local
concerns will map neatly onto teachers' and students' needs at other institutions.[2] The Michigan Tech case study can offer, however, an illustration of
the assessment model advocated by this book and a set of general assessment processes—although even these processes must be modified to suit
specific groups of students, teaching personnel, technologies, resources,
and the pedagogical realities of local institutions.

The goal of the model described in this chapter, as I suggested earlier,
is to democratize assessment and redesign. Five broad stages—or steps—
characterize the model:

> ▸ Step 1: Identify stakeholders,
> ▸ Step 2: Define issues and areas of interest on which to
>   focus,[3]
> ▸ Step 3: Observe current sites of effort and involvement,
> ▸ Step 4: Identify sites for increased involvement and invest-
>   ment, and
> ▸ Step 5: Pinpoint and fine-tunie involvement.

---

[2]Although I think readers will find that the design efforts we apply in an English
studies department at a technological university are remarkably applicable to most
educational institutions, K-college.

[3]The careful reader will probably ask herself, "Haven't I seen these first two stages
before? Isn't this what Selfe recommended way back in chapter 2 when he talked
about creating technology-rich environments?" Indeed it is. The cyclical nature of
creation and redesign makes these two processes very similar.

These assessment/redesign processes are highly recursive and very broadly defined. They are certainly not meant to solve problems in one sitting. To illustrate these processes, this chapter also provides readers three versions of an *assessment and redesign matrix*—like the one pictured in Figure 5.1 (see inserts).

Each version of the assessment/redesign matrix shares a common set of features:

- stakeholders' groups are listed vertically along the far left-hand column.
- issues or areas of interest are listed horizontally along the topmost row of the chart.
- cells represent the specific sites at which the experiences and activities of a particular group of stakeholders intersect with a particular issue or area of interest.

In terms of process, as indicated in Fig. 5.2, each of the three versions of the assessment and redesign matrix are keyed to stages or steps of the assessment model.

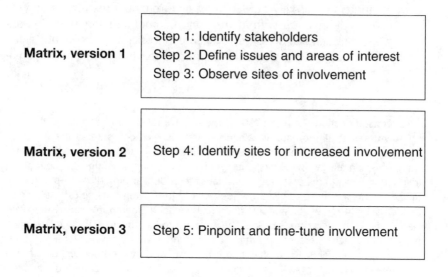

Figure 5.2   Three Versions of the Assessment and Redesign Matrix.

STEP 1: IDENTIFY STAKEHOLDERS

The first step that teachers need to think about in undertaking a formative process of assessing and redesigning technology-rich teaching and learning environments is constructing a broad map of the constituencies who might have some stake in these environments:

- students[4]
- teachers
- technical support people
- facility or site administrators
- program administrators
- student workers
- stakeholders outside the department

If English and language arts teachers have been following the larger process of user-based design outlined by this book, many of these constituencies have already been identified and involved in shaping computer-supported environments for communication (see chap. 2). These constituencies form a relatively stable core group of stakeholders who work with computers on a daily or weekly basis throughout the academic year and are directly involved with instruction in computer-supported environments. Not all stakeholders, however, are necessarily identifiable at all times during the life of a computer-supported teaching and learning envi-

---

[4]This constituency in the mid-1980s is the one we included accidentally, although by now it seems all too natural. When we first received computers from the computer science people in the same building, they came at the request of a programming philosopher, Dr. Bill Sewell. He was intent on programming computer-aided instructional programs that would facilitate the understanding of concepts that he taught. It was a noble and visionary idea that unfortunately was quickly subverted by increasing numbers of students and faculty who wandered into our closet-sized "lab" outside the secretary's office. They wanted to use this new thing called *word processing* (which operated on what was for then a very powerful type of "minicomputer" called TERAK). As has been the case with every other technology we have introduced in our facilities, students were the first ones to learn and teach the rest of us how to use each item. As a result of student suggestions, our next purchases were Macintoshes, and off we went. Student consultants still constitute one of our main bodies of interested stakeholders.

ronment—certainly many of them are not involved as such environments are coming into being and, as these environments change, various groups of stakeholders assume different profiles.

At Michigan Tech, for instance, after 15 years or so of operation in various forms, our assessment efforts indicate that our early list of stakeholders was neither exhaustive nor completely stable. The older our computer-supported environment grew, for example, the more actively we became involved with alumni of both our undergraduate and graduate programs. Students who had graduated from Michigan Tech's undergraduate programs—in Scientific and Technical Communication, Computer Science, Electrical Engineering, among other fields—had become valuable consultants about technical and procedural changes that we thought about making. They also began to identify technology-based internships for students both on and off campus, and to became active donors to the university and our programs. Individuals who had completed PhD and master degrees in Rhetoric and Technical Communication, meanwhile, had gone into industry or moved on to teach at other institutions. These alumni began to advise us on new technologies, the solutions other institutions had found to common technological or administrative problems, or software programs that did a better job of meeting student and faculty needs.

More recently, we have become involved in trying to extend our teaching and learning environments to better accommodate individuals with disabilities. As a result, we have entered conversations with colleagues at other institutions and software company representatives who can help us focus on meeting ADA requirements in our facilities and online systems.

Given these experiences, our evolving list of stakeholders is now periodically reviewed by members of our department's Computer Committee, by the undergraduate students and technical staff members who run our facilities, and by graduate students in our Rhetoric and Technical Communication program. This list changes regularly as new kinds of technological environments emerge, as we identify new issues and areas on which to focus, and as we involve different kinds of people in our continual efforts to design, assess, and redesign the computer-supported teaching and learning environments within which we work.

A recent list of stakeholders used for ongoing assessment and redesign efforts at MTU can be seen in Fig. 5.1. English and language arts teachers who work at other institutions and within other programs will of course want to identify their own lists of constituencies, including more people outside the immediate department, program, or school; or including different kinds of people within the institution's walls. K–12 English and language arts teachers who use computers are likely to recognize the importance of district-wide technology coordinators and grant writers, school board members, parent organizations, community organizations, and local corporations. In contrast, teachers at the collegiate level may want to tune their lists more finely within an institution. Many schools, for instance, have several types of teachers with differing constraints and needs: adjunct and part-time faculty, distance educators who may not even reside locally, and graduate student instructors.

One of the hardest cases to make to English studies and language arts professionals at workshops is the need to attend to institutional partners outside a department or division. Our training and responsibilities do not seem to encourage such collaborations. Although there are many reasons that we do not collaborate easily with members of our own institution, the sustainable practice described by Douglas Downs at the University of Utah is illustrative of why teachers of English and languages arts *should* be looking for and continuously refining relationships with groups outside their programs, academic units, and disciplines. His description is also an excellent argument for ongoing efforts of formative assessment—assessment that ascertains whether all the partners in a collaboration are benefiting from the activities that go on in a technology-rich teaching and learning environment.

A Sustainable Technology Collaboration between Library and Writing Program

Douglas Downs <d.downs@utah.edu>
University of Utah

The University of Utah's Marriott Library leads technology integration and teaching at the University. Perhaps the best example of sustainable practices is Marriott's collaboration with the University Writing Program, an independent department within the College of Humanities. The library collaborates with the writing program in three ways.

The first is information technology training in the UWP's "first-year" composition course, Writing 2010. Marriott's Instruction Division has for the last several years conducted training sessions for the annual 100+ sections of the course. The 2-hour sessions, conducted by librarians in collaboration with each course instructor, focus on using databases and other library technology in research.

The Instruction Division has always collected an evaluation form from students at the end of the instruction session; last year it built an electronic form linked to a database, which compiles information from student responses throughout the semester. The division also meets with 2010 instructors at the end of each semester to seek feedback and suggestions for curriculum revisions, and does the same with librarians who conduct the sessions. Together this feedback leads to curriculum changes almost every semester as the sessions change to match changes in the 2010 course and constantly changing technology. This assessment lends support to the notion that the instruction is both effective and necessary, helping to keep the sessions a fully budgeted priority that receives strong support from writing instructors, and making sure this technology instruction is fully sustainable.

Instructors of upper division writing courses also use the Instruction Division in teaching Web publishing and business writing. This assistance is usually in the form of short classes for students (1-4 hours long) in various programs and computer languages, although the Instruction Division will custom design course-integrated instruction for any request. As short classes are open to faculty as well, writing instructors find them useful in preparing themselves to teach the basics of electronic design and publishing.

On a larger scale, the university's Technology-Assisted Curriculum Center in the library is available to help instructors university-wide use classroom technology. This assistance varies from helping compose PowerPoint slide shows to setting up entire on-line courses. TACC also implements WebCT, which is heavily used within UWP courses. TACC thus gives instructors an easy, centralized source of technology help on demand. A number of things are being done right in this Marriott/UWP collaboration. The centralization and comprehensiveness of technology support offered by Marriott is wonderful. Instructors know where to go to have their questions answered directly and to get help with technology integration. Furthermore, locating that assistance within the university's center for information technology, the library is both intuitive and efficient. Most important, budgeting and staffing both the Instruction Division and TACC exemplifies a serious commitment to information technology and the training to use it.

Once regular funding and organizational structures exist, this technology assistance is sustained by the weight of faculty and student demand. Still that weight is simultaneously a threat to sustainability: The Instruction Division and TACC find themselves victims of their own success. As demand for course-integrated instruction increases, Marriott is simply running out of librarian hours and lab hours to fill the requests.

Thus, the Instruction Division and UWP are considering a "pass-it-on" design that would train writing instructors to conduct more technology instruction on their own. Such a design is particularly applicable to Writing 2010 instruction, one of the largest resource draws. The material this instruction covers is basic enough that writing instructors could achieve the same level of competence with it as the librarians who currently teach the sessions. Not only would using librarians to train 50 writing instructors per year to mastery of the material be much more sustainable than using librarians to train 2,500 students per year to familiarity with it, but doing so would also free librarians for course-integrated instruction that only they can do. Thinking and initiatives like these have brought this collaboration to sustainability and will ensure it as demand increases.

Successes

For 3 years now the UWP/MLID collaboration has been supported by a dedicated teaching assistant (TA) shared by the library and writing program. For the first 2 years this was funded by a special University Teaching Assistantship grant designed to pilot innovative teaching projects. The important news is that we were able to demonstrate the effectiveness of the position (in the writing program we call it the "library liaison") well enough that the library and writing program have taken over shared funding and made the position permanent. We did this through careful and extensive end-of-year reports the first two years (I was the first library liaison) that assessed the liaison's contribution to the university's, writing program's, and library's goals for improving information literacy among undergraduates at the university.

One final point about assessment: The library's instruction division never takes a step without it, and the data they can generate about the effects of any given program are an important source of information that helps sustain the program. They have been collecting self-reporting evaluations in the past, but are also developing a skills-querying evaluation that looks for improvements in various information-literacy skills during students' time at the university. If such evaluations demonstrate lots of learning, it makes the case for funding and cross-campus support even stronger.

This model is still in the thinking stages, although the need for it is becoming more pressing. Other departments across the university are, in part because of the success of the Instruction Division/UWP collaboration, increasingly seeking their own collaborations and course-integrated instruction.

- Links to further information on this collaboration: <http://www.lib.utah.edu/instruction>
- Fuller information about Marriott Library's Instruction Division, including its mission, all the courses it offers, and other services it provides. <http://www.lib.utah.edu/instruction/w2010/w2010.html>
- A page dedicated to Writing 2010, including both resources for the library instruction session and for research at Marriott Library. <http://www.tacc.utah.edu/>

In all of the situations mentioned in this section, the key questions driving this point of the assessment process are as follows:

- Who has a stake in computer-rich environments for teaching and learning English studies and language arts? What is at stake for each group?
- Who benefits from improving these environments?
- How can these individuals be convinced to join in ongoing design, redesign, and assessment efforts?

STEP 2: DEFINE ISSUES AND AREAS ON WHICH TO FOCUS

The second step of the assessment/redesign process outlined in this chapter involves English studies and language arts teachers in identifying the issues and areas of interest on which they want to focus their assessment efforts. In Fig. 5.1, readers can see a list of issues and areas that have formed the focus for the ongoing assessment efforts in Michigan Tech's CCLI in recent years. Perhaps the most important thing to understand about this list, however, does not show on the matrix—the list is always changing! New issues and areas of interest are always emerging as a computer-rich environment changes and grows and as the people who are part of this space exert their own shaping influences.

Some evidence of this process can be helpful here. The 1998 survey mentioned in the Preface to this book was designed to identify important sets of issue areas that were influencing institutions as they designed, implemented, and sustained technology-rich environments. From this research—and from subsequent workshops at MTU and other institutions—the following list of issues emerged as most important to *establishing* a technology-rich environment:

- instructional and curriculum design
- access
- technical support
- technology choices
- fiscal and material realities

This list of course did not prove to be stable. As our own computer-based environment matured, and as we learned more from other schools and institutions, additional issues that influenced the technological longevity of our systems emerged:

- professional development and recognition
- continuing fiscal management
- broadening and nurturing institutional relationships
- technological policy concerns
- long-term technology choices

Readers may notice that *technology choices* is the last issue on each list. Normally, and unfortunately, it is usually the first and often the *only* issue to be discussed at meetings about technology-rich environments. Because of this tendency, we did not include the issue of technology on the assessment redesign matrixes. We learned early in the process of sustaining computer-rich environments that technological choices get constant attention from stakeholders without even being formally included in the assessment effort. Almost everybody involved in running the CCLI, for instance, asked questions like the following: What versions of which software should we buy? How much do they cost? How do we install and maintain them? What are they compatible and incompatible with? Who has access to them and when? What activities do our online interfaces encourage and discourage?

In the context of this ongoing conversation, we decided that technology should remain in the background of our attention—even during assessment and redesign. Instead we decided to focus our assessment attention on what we considered (and still do) more important matters—human and social issues, issues of design and interaction, learning, and levels of involvement that would help English studies and language arts profession-als, students, staff, and administrators create a locally sustainable culture of support and reduce the roar of the bits and bytes discussions to a rea-sonable level.

The lesson for readers in this case is that issues and areas are a func-tion of local conditions and can, thus, be identified only by the stakeholders involved in an assessment effort. By committing themselves to involvement in such efforts, instead of leaving technology decisions and assessment up to technology experts, English and language arts teachers can assure that humanistic issues and areas of interest are centrally represented.

STEP 3: IDENTIFY SPECIFIC SITES OF EFFORT AND INVOLVEMENT

The third step of our formative assessment and redesign process involves filling in the individuals cells of the matrix as shown in Fig. 5.1—focusing, at this point, on identifying ways in which members of each stakeholder group involve themselves (or not) in specific issues or areas of interest.

This activity is designed to reveal three things:

1. *which issues groups of stakeholders currently consider most important* (i.e., issues on which they choose to spend their time and effort),
2. a systematic snapshot of *how groups of stakeholders are involved* in particular issues or areas of interest (i.e., in what specific activities are they actually engaged?), and
3. *the level of involvement that each group* has in each issue or area of interest.

In addition, the activity suggests the specific kinds and levels of responsi-bilities that members of each group can assume in a user-based redesign project.

When the Michigan Tech team engaged in this step of the process, for example, the student users of the CCLI indicated that their involvement in helping to design effective computer-supported instruction was limited to those few occasions when they were asked to evaluate the lab component of computer-intensive (CI) classes and those times when they reported system bottlenecks to the teachers of these classes. The representation of this situation can be seen in Fig. 5.3 in the cell at the intersection of row labeled "students" and the column entitled "Instruction Design." On the Likert scale at the bottom of this cell, students rated their involvement at a relatively low level.

In the second cell of that same column (at the intersection of the column labeled "instructional design" and the row labeled "teachers"), teachers reported efforts in designing computer-intensive courses and designing the weekly teaching with information technology (TWIT) sessions offered in the department. For these reasons, the assessment team rated their level of involvement at a relatively high level.

In the third cell of the same column (see Fig. 5.1: at the intersection of the column labeled "instructional design" and the row labeled "technical support people"), members of the technical support staff noted that their involvement in instructional design was limited to receiving feedback

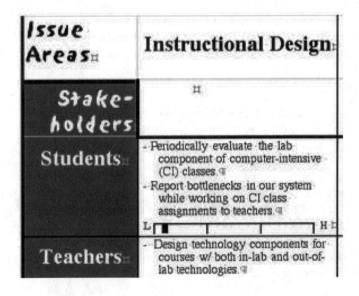

Figure 5.3 Identifying Current Sites of Effort and Involvement in the Cells of the Assessment/Redesign Matrix, Version 1

from faculty who taught computer-intensive courses and attending some weekly TWIT meetings. The assessment team rated their level of involvement relatively low.

Because this step of the assessment process provides a systematic snapshot of current sites and levels of involvement, it generates a great deal of valuable information for English and language arts teachers concerned about how computer-rich environments operate, who is involved, and what efforts are being expended in sustaining these environments. As the first version of the matrix is completed—and all the cells are slowly filled in—the processes of discussing and analyzing the information has already begun.

Using the completed matrix, the assessment team can also analyze the current status of stakeholder involvement in a technology-rich environment, evaluate whether these levels of involvement are satisfactory within the context of the environment's goals, and begin to forecast possible areas of *redesign*—areas in which the assessment team wants to improve the level of stakeholders' involvement and, through this involvement, assure that the technology-rich environment will do a better job of meeting their needs.

This set of tasks—identifying not only where the program is most successful, but also where change is most needed—may require several close readings of, and discussions about, a completed matrix. The goal of such readings and discussions is not only to identify how stakeholders and groups are *currently* engaged in shaping computer-rich environments, a form of technological activism, but also how they *might be engaged more fully or completely in the future.*

In discussions at this stage, the CCLI team learned, that students were quite willing to be more closely involved in the design of computer-based instruction—in user testing such instruction, helping teachers identify the best courses and activities in which to integrate technology, and researching software packages that might help in such efforts. The team also learned that technical staff members were willing to increase their involvement in the effort to design effective computer-based instruction by offering additional TWIT (teaching with information technology) sessions on system constraints and opportunities with which teachers were still unfamiliar.

For the purposes of forecasting redesign efforts, the first version of the assessment/redesign matrix can be read both vertically and horizontally. At MTU, for instance, we used the different stakeholders' comments in the column labeled *access* (Fig. 5.1) to complicate our understanding of that term and what people normally mean by it. The results of that vertical reading effort (as well as our workshop experiences at other institutions) led to 11 practical and immediate action items that we have tried to implement at MTU (see Appendix 5.1: Redefining Access). The long-term effect of these action items helped re-create the culture of support for students and teachers who wished to work with new *and* well-established technologies in the Humanities Department at MTU.

The cells of the assessment and redesign matrix can also be read horizontally. For instance, when the CCLI team noticed a consistently low level of student involvement across all issues and interest areas (the row labeled *students* in Fig. 5.1), they focused their efforts on addressing this situation—inviting more students to become consultants within the CCLI, seeking student input on the design and redesign of technology-rich systems and classes, inviting students to attend TWIT sessions, increasing the number of opportunities for students to evaluate CI classes, and creating an online suggestion box.

The Michigan Tech team also found that discussions happening during this stage of the assessment/redesign process served to support the formation of community within the CCLI—especially over time. We not only provided stakeholders an opportunity to frame issues discursively and identify their own strategies for being involved in computer-supported environments, these discussions also allowed literacy professionals an additional opportunity to increase the involvement of various stakeholders groups in the ongoing design of this environment. They were, in fact, using technological change to build community.

STEP 4: IDENTIFY SITES FOR INCREASED INVOLVEMENT AND INVESTMENT

In the fourth step of the process, the assessment team uses the information gathered during Steps 1 to 3 to outline a range of opportunities, activities, and events—I'll call them *sites*—that will help increase stakeholder involvement and investment in a computer-rich teaching and learning environment. During this stage, the assessment team determines how to set about the process of redesign most productively, how to coordinate and prioritize efforts to change technical practices and environments, and how to involve stakeholders more thoughtfully and in more meaningful ways. To make sure they approach redesign in a systematic way, the assessment team should also draft a second version of the matrix in which they identify possible ways of taking better advantage of the expertise and perspective of stakeholders.

Figure 5.4, for instance, shows a second version of the assessment/redesign matrix (see inserts). This version was constructed by the CCLI team after the first version of the assessment and redesign matrix had been completed and analyzed. The team compiled this second version to identify in a systematic way the user-based redesign efforts that they wanted to carry out in the Humanities Department. This second version of the matrix was not meant to serve as *a* snapshot of *what was* (like the first version of the matrix), but rather it represented *what could be*. It provided a blueprint for redesign activities.

Read horizontally across the *student* row of cells, for instance, the second matrix (Fig. 5.4) identifies a set of activities that the CCLI assessment team at Michigan Tech thought would increase the involvement and investment of students in our computer-supported teaching and learning environment. In addition, the matrix suggests, in most cases, the responsibilities assigned to stakeholders for implementing those activities.

This second matrix is both dynamic and cumulative—it does not have to be re-created from scratch each time a different group is brought together or a slightly new but related issue comes up. New groups of stakeholders can—and should—be added. Similarly, issues that are no longer a priority can be removed. Thus, if the first version of the assessment matrix represents a static snapshot of how stakeholders are involved in a computer-supported environment at *a particular point in time,* the second matrix represents a dynamic list of possible projects and activities designed to help reinvigorate a particular technology-rich environment *over time.*

In this context, it is important to note that although every activity on this list adds to the culture of support necessary to sustain technology-rich instruction, the entire list cannot be accomplished or addressed at once or even in the course of one academic year. For an assessment team, the primary goal of filling out this second matrix should be to choose the most important, immediate, and productive action items for a particular institution or program. Their job is to select and prioritize what needs to be done immediately and what must wait for later so that technology stakeholders do not burn out and so computer-based efforts can be sustained over time.

At Nothern Illinois University (NIU), English faculty use specific communication-related instructional goals and institutional mandates in designing and redesigning both their technology-rich environments and the system of instructional support that underlies those environments. The assessment efforts at NIU are closely related, as this chapter has suggested, to the needs of teachers and students and to the pedagogical goals of the department. These efforts are shaped, further, by both the instructional and fiscal responsibilities the department has within the larger university community. K–12 professionals may want to review this sustainable practice as a way to anticipate the expectations that many first-year composition programs now have for college-bound students.

Computer Assisted First-Year Composition at Northern Illinois University

Michael Day (contact person) <mday@niu.edu>
Eric Hoffman
Robert Self

Because computers have become the main tools for writing and the Internet a major medium for disseminating writing, many first-year composition programs have met the challenge of changing media by scheduling at least some classes in networked computer labs. The First-Year Composition Program at NIU continues to blaze the trail of technology integration, requiring that all first-year composition classes (about 150 sections each semester with 3000 students) meet at least 1 day a week in a computer lab. In addition, the new first-year composition teaching assistants at NIU actively and collaboratively develop ways to enhance their classes using computer-mediated communication.

In requiring the computer lab component, NIU's composition program assumes that college students should develop technological literacy in context; that is, when technology can be used appropriately at the service of other needs, such as writing. Because so much writing is created on computers and/or has migrated online, the first-year composition class becomes the logical place for students to learn to use computers and the Internet. This requirement by the university motivated its commitment of the financial resources necessary to build seven computer laboratories to support computer-mediated instruction in English core competency courses.

As is true at many schools, all of our students can log in to the campus network, and all can use e-mail and the World Wide Web. But one aspect that sets us apart from many other schools using commercial course packages such as BlackBoard and WebCT is our suite of class management and discussion tools especially designed for composition classes. As commercial "one size fits all" course management systems

become ubiquitous, and courseware tends to drive pedagogical decisions, the more composition programs need customized environments
based on pedagogical practice and not ease of design. Our program
uses a combination of commercial and open source software to provide
customized templates and resources for teachers and students. These
customized environments are, above all, predicated by pedagogy and
are designed to assist us in reaching our overall goals of helping students write better and helping them acclimate to the electronic environment as a site of written communication.

More specifically, we believe that by the end of our 1-year first-year
composition sequence, students should be able to

▸ use a word processor to revise and format texts, compare
  drafts, and save texts as HTML documents
▸ evaluate, properly incorporate, and cite material from outside
  webbed sources in research projects
▸ use e-mail, asynchronous discussion software, and chat rooms to
  brainstorm ideas, provide feedback, and keep in touch with the
  class
▸ understand the basics of netiquette and the dynamics of online (as
  compared to print-based) communication
▸ utilize electronic documentation (how to find help)

Our first-year teaching assistants (TAs) attend a full-year, 6-hour
graduate course, Seminar in the Teaching of College Writing, which
includes one class per week in the computer lab preparing them to
teach the lab sections of their classes. Through hands-on experience
with the tools, collaborating with each other on lab assignments, and
consulting with veteran tech-savvy teachers, the TAs develop confidence
in an approach to teaching composition informed by the latest and best
of computers and writing research.

Our TA pedagogy class is complemented by a teacher-training lab,
which doubles as a graduate classroom. This "Networked Writing and
Research" lab is run by a full-time faculty member who helps co-teach
the training seminar and is staffed with more experienced graduate students and instructors. The presence of this lab keeps discussions and
applications of technology integration very active in the department and
reinforces the culture of human support, which lies at the center of our
successful operation.

One unexpected benefit of this arrangement is the advanced level of
technology training that we can provide the graduate students who work

in the lab, preparing them for careers that more and more often will demand computer and Internet expertise. The university developed a fee structure several years ago to support its mission to integrate computer literacy into the curriculum; a portion of that fee directly supports the computer labs—the hardware, software, personnel, and teacher training—dedicated to the university's 6-hour general education requirement of rhetoric and composition.

Our current level of technology integration is economically sustainable, even in these times of shrinking budgets, because we can guarantee to the university that not only do we help it fulfill its mission to improve communication skills, we can also guarantee that its graduates will be able to use current computer and Internet technologies, particularly those used for writing and communication. That commitment, on a scale that reaches every undergraduate at our school through required core competency classes, ensures that we will continue to be able to schedule first-year composition classes in our dedicated labs at least 1 day a week.

We are currently developing a programmatic assessment process and would like to obtain as much feedback on the effectiveness of our uses of computer technology in the program as we can. With this goal in mind, we are designing entrance and exit questionnaires on computer skills and attitudes to be administered electronically for each first-year composition class, and we are looking into the possibility of testing students' computerized writing abilities when they enter and exit our program. We believe that it is only by collecting rich data on attitudes and abilities that we can assess how well we are meeting our program goals.

In the future, we would like to move in two directions. First, we hope to develop a pilot program for incorporating webbed portfolios (webfolios) in first-year composition classes through the classes of the TAs in our pedagogy seminar. Second, we would like to extend our TA training for computer-assisted writing to the campus Writing Across the Curriculum program by offering a technology-rich composition pedagogy class for TAs in other departments who would become writing consultants for courses in those departments.

For further explanation, browse through more resources and project descriptions at the following URLs:

- First-year composition home page:
  http://www.engl.niu.edu/fycomp
- Department of English home page:
  http://www.engl.niu.edu/NIU home page: http://www.niu.edu

STEP 5: PINPOINT AND FINE-TUNE INVOLVEMENT

In the fifth step of the recursive assessment process outlined by this chapter, assessment team members pinpoint and fine-tune the opportunities for stakeholders to become involved in user-based redesign efforts—getting increasingly specific about the ways in which to get interested individuals involved at *particular moments of time* and in *specific institutional contexts.* The goal at this stage is to identify, for a wide range of stakeholders, a set of specific, concrete, and, if possible, convenient moments of intervention: that is, opportunities to provide important feedback and perspective without necessarily committing these stakeholders to long-term investments in time and effort. Figure 5.5 shows a third version of the assessment and redesign matrix focused on this particular step.

To illustrate the importance of this third version of the matrix, I offer a final example of Michgan Tech's efforts, referring to Fig. 5.5 (see inserts). Reading horizontally along the first row of cells labeled *students,* because we wanted to increase the level of student involvement in the financial operations of the CCLI, we needed to pinpoint events, times, places, and activities that would give them this opportunity. The team decided to focus on the task of getting students to attend the meetings where decisions about computer lab-fee levels were made. To be effective in increasing the level of student involvement in this activity, the team had to identify the times and places of the meetings, and we needed to encourage students to send representatives to these meetings willing to participate actively in discussing and making decisions about such fees.

This specific moment of intervention and involvement—now an established part of the lab-fee approval process at MTU—had to be explicitly pinpointed and fine-tuned for students before they could take advantage of it.

The task of successfully identifying specific opportunities and venues for the increased involvement of other stakeholders is not an easy one. Assessment team members need to be especially diligent about providing convenient ways in which participants can become involved in the process of user-based redesign without becoming overburdened and burning out. This effort is perhaps *the* most important component of establishing sustainable technology-rich systems in English studies and language arts departments and one of the hardest to do well.

The reasons for this situation are clear. Every department and school in the country is somewhere in the process of either initiating or reinvigorating its approach to technology-rich instruction; many are being asked to help develop distance education programs, put computers into classrooms, develop online systems, and network buildings, build labs and "smart" classrooms, buy new software, set up and send faculty and staff off to workshops, and so on. However, the pace of technological change, and thus the need to attend to technology issues, will only *increase* over the coming decades. In facing such challenges, we all have to become increasingly selective about involving ourselves and others in the user-based design and redesign of computer-supported teaching and learning environments. This context underscores the need for assessment/redesign teams to pinpoint and fine-tune the specific sites for stakeholders' involvement so that they are practical, short-lived, and of particular tactical importance.

The chart in Fig. 5.6 offers an example of this process. It demonstrates how the involvement of various stakeholders in an English department might be pinpointed and fine-tuned within the context of institution-wide technology initiatives. Readers should note the series of questions that help identify specific sites and approaches to involvement—practical, tactical, and short-lived—fleeting moments of involvement, rather than life-long commitments.

K–12 educators may be faced with different school-wide initiatives or identify different tactical moments for stakeholders' involvement, but the basic principles remain the same: students, teachers, staff members, and administrators can all learn from opportunities to make decisions about technology, and they can make important contributions—especially as institutional technology projects are formulated. It is important, however, to maintain sustainable technology efforts by making sure that willing activists do not spend time and energy on projects that are unfocused or overly broad.

Most English studies and language arts programs also have the ability to connect these moments of involvement to institutionalized systems of reward. Faculty who design courses (row one, right-most cell of Fig. 5.5) and serve on committees (row six, right-most cell), for instance, can be rewarded with recognition of their teaching and service contributions at tenure and promotion time. Students who try classroom assignments in new computer-rich environments (row six, the right-most cell) can be assigned extra credit or independent study credit for their contributions; graduate students who offer workshops of computer-based approaches (row five, right-most cell) can be rewarded with letters of recommendation for their dossiers.

Finally, consider the position of local technology support people. The last step of the assessment/redesign process (although there really is no first or last step, given that the process is ongoing and recursive) can prove one of the most useful *and* politically charged stages—especially if the scope of the decision-making team for a computer-based environment has been artificially limited until this point. When an assessment team commits to publishing a plan (like Fig. 5.5) for increasing stakeholders' involvement in computer-supported teaching and learning environments—and carrying out that plan—they also make a public statement about the depth and breadth of their efforts to democratize technological decision making. In most cases, individuals (e.g., system administrators) or technology teams responsible for administering computer-supported teaching and learning facilities are not trying to control the systems for which they are responsible. Rather, they have been left to survive on their own for so long that they have become unused to anyone else caring about the mundane, but essential, issues that come up on a daily basis. If at all possible, technology support people—who have often in the past been asked to carry on the planning of computer-supported systems entirely on their own—need to be intimately involved in the development of these assessment efforts and planning documents created by these multistakeholder assessment teams.

INSTITUTIONAL TECHNOLOGY INITIATIVES	QUESTIONS	MOMENTS OF TACTICAL INVOLVEMENT
An institutional initiative to create distance or hybrid courses.	Which classes should be taught at a distance? How will they be taught? When will they be designed? By whom?	. . . when a new course is being designed in the English department; collaborate with a member of the curriculum committee to design a hybrid version of this course. . . . when colleagues are preparing to teach a familiar course, help them design one new computer-supported instructional activity into its fabric.
An institutional initiative provide computers to all	What sort of computers do students need? Who will decide this? When and where will this decision be made?	. . . when a survey is compiled to send out to students or faculty; ask English students what they think. . . . when the institutional committee meets.
An institutional initiative to network buildings	What levels of access to networks (including speed of access) are appropriate for students and teachers in English studies and Language arts? Who will decide this? When and where will the decision be made? How?	. . . when the initial planning meetings for networking are taking place; ask your lab's system administrator and knowledgable faculty to talk to the committee about the English department's networking needs.

**Figure 5.6 Identifying Tactical Moments for Involvement in
           Technological Projects**

INSTITUTIONAL TECHNOLOGY INITIATIVES	QUESTIONS	MOMENTS OF TACTICAL INVOLVEMENT
An institutional initiative to develop labs and smart classrooms	What physical and virtual architectures make sense for labs and smart classrooms used by teachers? Who will decide on the configuration of labs? Smart classrooms? When and where will the decisions be made? How?	. . . when technological models are being discussed, confer with colleagues at other institutions to find out what they have done to support the teaching of English and language arts. . . . on e-mail ask Engish colleagues to imagine an ideal classroom for the courses they teach.
An institutional initiative to provide technology workshops	What activities are most useful to the attendees of those workshops—especially in English and language arts? Who will decide what workshops to offer? When and where will the decision be made?	. . . when workshop designers are soliciting suggestions, ask graduate teaching assistants in the department to suggest workshops they need in the area of computer-supported communication. . . . ask graduate stu dents who work in a departmental computer lab to offer workshops focused on the specific instructional needs of English and language arts students and teachers.
An institutional initiative to adopt computer-based course management program like Blackboard or WebCT.	Who is this system intended for? Who will decide what workshops to offer? When and where will the decision be ? How?	. . . when the campus committee is being formed, ask a colleague from English to volunteer; . . . ask a computer-savvy student to try out a specific class activity to identify the strengths and weaknesses of the environment.

WHY SUCH A COMPLEX EFFORT?

The five-step process of formative assessment outlined in this chapter is directed primarily at assessing the involvement level of stakeholders in technology-rich environments and, based on this assessment, making changes in the environment that better address the needs of all users (students, teachers, administrators). The process is recursive. Each year or so, an assessment team needs to revisit the list of stakeholders and issue areas and reassess the levels of involvement as a result of the planning and implementation that followed the development of Versions 2 and 3 of the assessment and redesign matrixes. Finally, Matrixes 2 and 3 need to be revisited. The weekly (or otherwise periodic) discussions that result will provide a rich and stable context for the "bits and bytes" discussions that must also occur. The result should be to infuse a healthy dose of human and pedagogical concerns into the technological discussions that go into maintaining these instructional environments. This sustaining assessment and redesign process has other outcomes as well.

Those who do become involved in the process, for instance, train themselves to take on a role as technological activists: folks who manage and shape technological change rather than simply falling prey to it. Further, stakeholders who participate in such an assessment/redesign effort become much more aware of the constraints and conditions under which other people work with technology. As a result, they also become far less likely to participate in the dynamic of blame that exists in many forms and in many departments, institutions, and communities. In other words, the kind of assessment and redesign effort described in this book can help produce increasingly effective activist citizens—individuals better prepared to deal with the technological changes they will face in schools, in the workplace, and at home in the coming decades.

Unfortunately, because of the complex, ongoing nature of assessing and redesigning technology-rich environments, some English and language arts educators will ask whether such an effort should not be left to more technically minded specialists. As a profession, however, we cannot afford to abdicate our responsibility for paying close attention to the important details of designing and operating the technological environments within which new forms of literacy are being practiced and on which we depend for the teaching of literacy. Access to the details of designing, operating, and sustaining such environments determines, fundamentally, our ability to act as effective agents of change within such environments. If we allow technical specialists to determine the design and operation of technology-rich environments for literacy teaching and learning on their own, we get environments made to the specifications of technicians, not environments that answer the needs of teachers and students who are studying English and the language arts.

Andrew Feenberg refers to the kinds of assessment and redesign projects identified in this chapter as *underdetermined* sites of design potential.[5] To make these sites work for us—to more effectively determine their constitution and goals, their size and shape and values, their democratic potential—English and language arts teachers need to open up the decision-making processes within them to the widest possible range of stakeholders. One outcome of such efforts—if we undertake them thoughtfully and carefully—will be multiplication of sustainable technological environments that are shaped by humanist values and informed by the practice of communication.

---

[5]See Feenberg's (1997) interesting analysis of agency and technology in Alternative Modernities.

AFTERWORD

FINAL SUMMARY AND COMMENTS

The intent of this volume is to provide English studies and language arts professionals with strategies for managing—in a critical, active, and productive way—the demands of the technology-rich teaching and learning environments on which we now depend. By joining, leading, or working with a team of interested stakeholders, English and language arts teachers can minimize the dynamic of blame that often develops in a community of technology users. If this effort is careful and systematic and sustained over time, the team becomes more than a group of technology *advocates*. Instead it develops into a knowledgeable team of technology *activists*—an integral part of a local culture of support that continues to address the learning requirements of students (people first), the instructional concerns of teachers (pedagogy second) and the technological conditions of the systems on which we have all come to depend (technology third).

I have suggested that this team of primary stakeholders can begin such an effort by designing a culture that will support teachers as they learn new technologies, plan for their use, implement computer-supported lessons in classes, assess the effectiveness of instruction, and revise instruction accordingly. Cultures of support, shaped by local conditions and practices, can help teachers and students by assembling collections of successful technology-rich lesson plans, offering formal and informal workshops, and involving stakeholder groups in making decisions about technology.

In these workshops and meetings, stakeholders, in general—and English-language arts teachers more specifically—can learn how to identify the complex set of constraints and expectations under which technology-rich instruction operates. They can also learn how to address, in increasingly productive ways, the social, curricular, political, institutional, economic, and technical issues associated with technology use. Perhaps most importantly, team members can learn, through first-hand experience, how they can sustain the various components of a culture of support:

- Robust technical environments (physical and digital) for teachers and students,
- a student technology assistant program,
- a range of technology-rich professional development opportunities, and
- a sound financial plan that includes an amortized budget.

This book has also provided suggestions for English and language arts teachers already involved in administering and operating computer-rich teaching and learning facilities. With the assessment-redesign process outlined in Chapter 5, technology leaders can begin to identify and address systematically the issues that characterize computer-rich instructional environments. By creating their version of the assessment and redesign matrices provided in this book, teachers can document how engaged stakeholders are in the design and redesign of computer-rich environments (version one of the matrix), identify the key areas in which the involvement might be improved (version two of the matrix), and identify opportunities of increased—and increasingly effective—involvement (version three).

Through these processes of design, assessment, and redesign teachers of English and language arts do more than address the practical "bits and bytes" decisions of computer-supported teaching in a timely manner. They also become involved in creating what Brown and Duguid call (following the lead of Lave and Wegner) a community of practice: a group of tightly knit individuals so steeped in the intersections of pedagogy and technology that they can succeed in managing complex environments of computer-supported instruction (pp. 142-143).

One of the great, and often unacknowledged, values of engaging in this type of technological activism, is that English studies and language arts teachers contribute to the formation of communities that reach out beyond the institution and affect our larger technological culture. Although there are plenty of popular technology critics who describe in detail how new technologies are dismantling our local communities, few provide suggestions about how to bring people together in order to manage and shape technological environments proactively. This book identifies a series of team-based opportunities for developing and sustaining activist habits of mind in relation to technology.

This effort is not easy, nor is it simple. But English and language arts teachers already know the risks they face if they choose inaction over involvement, an increasing dynamic of blame that develops around the process of technology design. As Paul LeBlanc, President of Marlboro College at the time, notes teachers cannot be effective advocates for their technology needs unless they can also communicate their vision of productive directions for computer-based instruction:

> We need to reframe our approach to administrators, to supply them with the ammunition they need to get us resources. If we simply go to them with "I need" pleas; well . . . get in line. They hear that all day long. We are, as a community, doing exciting and often groundbreaking work, but we seek support like paupers at the gate. (personal correspondence, February 17, 1997)

The project of designing and sustaining educational environments in which teachers and students can use computers effectively to learn about language and to engage in the practices of literacy is a complicated business that requires the input of technical specialists, content specialists, computer users, administrators, parents, alumni, and community members. Teachers of English and language arts cannot hope to manage such environments alone, nor can we succeed if we ignore our responsibility for their design and operation, if we refuse to pay attention to the changing nature of language values and practices in such spaces.

It is only by assembling talented teams of stakeholders that we can lead departments and schools toward more appropriate and humanistic uses of communication technologies. These teams are capable of contributing an astonishing amount of energy and spirit to our project. They can also help make the job of teaching increasingly productive, challenging, and engaging. With the help of these teams, we can re-imagine how humans relate effectively to technology and to each other. What more can we ask of a job or a community?

Appendix 2.1

TECHNO-PEDAGOGICAL
EXPLORATIONS

TOWARD SUSTAINABLE TECHNOLOGY-RICH INSTRUCTION

This is not a book about pedagogy or instructional design per se, but those reading this collection are probably considering how they might, appropriately, integrate sustainable[1] technologies into their pedagogy. With that in mind, I included this shortened version of a chapter I published in Takayoshi and Huot's recent *Teaching Writing with Computers: An Introduction*.

Perhaps you've been convinced by Cindy Selfe's warnings about NOT paying attention to technology and the need to develop critical technological literacies for the 21st century (cf. Selfe, 1999)? Or maybe you've been arm wrestled into taking on a hybrid (partially online and partially face-to-face) course or a class taught at a distance (cf. DeVoss, Hayden, Selfe, & Selfe, 2001). Perhaps you've read or seen exciting applications of communication technologies in workshops or other classes and want to experiment yourself. Perhaps communication technologies just seem like an inevitable, "natural" part of the modern landscape, and you can't imagine *not* enacting that part of the culture in your class. (Many people apply words like overdetermination (cf. Feenberg) and ideology (cf. Eagleton) to this sort of observation. Eagleton and Feenberg provide useful theoretical approaches

---

[1]The word "sustainable" has a wealth of meaning for me (R. Selfe, 1998). Essentially, we want locally sustainable technologies because we can't afford to invest time and money in instructional systems that will change over night; because successful teachers explore technology-rich pedagogy over a long period of time; and because these efforts should be tied intimately to changes in our understandings of literacy and learning, neither of which are stable (see the section "All technology-rich pedagogy is experimental" for more justification of sustainability).

(Published first in *Teaching Writing With Computers: An Introduction*, Pam Takayoshi & Brian Huot, eds. Boston: Houghton Mifflin Co., 2003, 17-32.)

to these concepts.). Whatever interests teachers bring to this task, I have found the following set of reminders of great use to the faculty, staff and graduate students that I've worked with over the years. Indeed, I have to reconsider them myself each year, each term, and each time I teaching with technology:

- All technology-rich (TR) pedagogy is experimental.
- Develop locally sustainable teaching practices.
- Don't let the technologies themselves drive your pedagogy,

   unless . . .

- Get to know your students.
- Sequence your assignments.
- Assess what you do as you go.
- Don't take yourself and your efforts too seriously.
- For each TR experiment, use the PAR system (preparation, activity, reflection).
- Add a "critical component" to each lesson.
- Network (in the interpersonal sense) with those around you:
  ‣ Talk to great teachers from all disciplines and collaborate with them.
  ‣ Recruit students as technology assistants for the next round of teaching with technology (TWT).
  ‣ Share your insights with other scholar/teachers.

Though these "reminders" can be read in any order, they do tend to build on each other. In the full chapter version of this piece (Selfe, 2003), I've included, with the short justification for each claim, several supplemental items:

- a techno-pedagogical exploration (an overview of a technology-rich lesson),
- a short description of the technology itself,
- some additional characteristics of the technology being considered, and finally,
- a warning about the technology itself or the activity I'm proposing.

All technology-rich pedagogy is experimental.

How can this be? English studies scholar/teachers have been at this since the early 1980s! The fact is that the interface or interfaces that we use, students' lives, access levels, the underlying networks, people's placement on the technological learning curve, the material conditions that surround the class and students, the curriculum, and everyone's expectations are all unstable and changing term-by-term, sometimes class session by class session. I have to remind myself of this fact every day and confront students with the experimental nature of teaching with technology (TWT). I do this in order to engage them in the experiment. As a teacher that's part of my responsibility along with the need to attend to students' techno-pedagogical experiences as carefully (though maybe not as often) as I do their literacy needs. After all, the two (literacy and technology) are intimately connected (see Chapter 1).

Some of these strategies (that I've used in the past) help control the instabilities and some use those instabilities to the class' advantage.

Commit yourself to developing locally sustainable teaching practices.

In order to sustain your own interest and commitment, imagine practical pedagogical objectives that you believe a communication technology(ies) might help you accomplish, one that is difficult to accomplish in your 'traditional' class (however you define 'traditional'). Then apply a structured use of the technology to that objective; watch how the community of students react to your approach, and let them help you redesign the approach to better accomplish the objective the next time. Let students in on your "objectives," and explain them over and over during the term. This is experimental work, they aren't used to teachers being so up front with them, and, in my experience, they won't "get it" unless you keep reframing it for them as the term progresses.

A Negative Corollary: Don't simply engage in a technology exploration because you've heard of or seen interesting things happen in other teachers' classes unless . . . unless you and the students enter that digital space together, explicitly as explorers.

Early adopters of technologies have usually developed sustainable pedagogies over a number of years. They are also notorious (myself included) for telling only half the story in descriptions of their and their students' experiences: these often include only a few of the motivations at work, a smattering of details about the material conditions under which they work, and a couple of the steps they took to ensure success (when, actually, there might be 20 steps or more, some of which they may not be able to articulate!). This is why online and local mentoring is so important and another reason why those new to technology-rich instruction will find the process so experimental. However, over the years you are quite likely to see demonstrations of, hear about, or have new technologies imposed on you that seem to have pedagogical promise. In addition, you may not have local or online mentors willing to help in the step-by-step process of developing sustainable teaching practices around that technology.

So, each term, I see no reason why we all shouldn't experiment with the use of one technology or technology-rich activity that is new if you and your students as long as you both enter that activity in exploratory mode.

Get to know your students and their technological attitudes, abilities, and their expectations for technology-rich instruction.

Assign technology autobiographies (cf. Kitalong et al.). Our students come from wildly divergent technological backgrounds even in relatively homogeneous populations. And their experiences are not stable from one term to the next. The more we know about our students' past as we integrate technologies into the curriculum, the better. So, early in the term, have them write about their technological experiences. Or as I suggest below, have them compose "media representations" of those experiences. Here are a few of the typical questions that my colleagues and I have had success with in the past:

- What were your earliest experiences with technological devices or artifacts? What were they? What do you remember about using them?
- What gadgets were popular in your house while you were growing up?
- Who do you identify as being technologically "literate" in your life? What does it mean to be technologically literate? How do you measure up?
- What technologies are on your desk at home? What technological devices are you carrying now? What's on your technological "wish list"?

- How do your experiences differ from those of your older brothers and sisters, your parents, your grandparents? (You may wish to interview older members of your family to learn about their technological memories.)
- How do you see technology as a force in the future, either in your career or personal life?
- What are your technological strengths? What technology outside of class do you have access to that might be useful in this course? How willing are you to incorporate teaching into the course requirements of the class: that is, take on the job of being the technical expert for novices in the class?
- What image best represents a computer or computer network to you (other than the computer itself)?
"A computer is like a _____."
"A computer is a _____."

Please elaborate: why do you say this? In what specific ways is it true? Please sketch your favorite image below.

Sequence Assignments

One-time activities involving technologies are almost never of great valuable in and of themselves. That's why workshops that give teachers one-time experiences can really never match or be highly predictive of what actually goes on in classes over time. The systematic use of a technology over time is an experiment in and of itself. I keep reminding myself that the technology experience of my students has to be part of an on-going set of events that feed into each other.

For instance,
we might read a novel and discuss it online. = >
They bring in their favorite posts to spark further discussions in class. = >
This then leads to the viewing of a related movie. = >
During that movie I might explore the use of a synchronous discussion to "take notes." = >
And in turn, I might then have the students review the log of that chat session in order to separate out the chaff from the wheat, (or in the parlance from my part of the country, the gems from the clinkers) and report back to the class.
Sequenced assignments with purpose and follow-up have always worked more effectively in my classes.

Have some way of assessing technically mediated assignments—not just students' compositions— incrementally over the term.

When *you* assess student compositions, have *them* assess the technology-rich activities that led up to their final draft. For instance there are ways of creating a dialogue between students and teachers if one has access to technologies like email list software. With this software you can "assess" any aspect of your class during the term, including techno-pedagogical activities by setting up an email list with a name something like this: techno-assess-L@genericU.edu (the name is typically not case sensitive). After setting up the list and subscribing students, the forum can be used for holding open discussions about the technology components used in the class. Teachers can choose not to be involved at all (collect mail unread throughout the term until after grades are in), or they can be readers of student comments or an active participant in the discussion. Open discussions are interesting and often quite blunt. I try to warn teachers new to these technologies that if you ask students to comment honestly, expect them to do just that. We aren't always going to like what students have to say. I have gathered some evidence from many past list discussion that this environment is *not* well suited to "coming to consensus." Instead, email lists often promote dissensual conversations containing many issues that remain unresolved. Students need to be made aware of this as well. That's why I suggested using email lists along with more anonymous methods of assessment. In this case I might ask students to discuss pros and cons of a particular activity on the list and then submit an anonymous paper copy of their final comments to me individually after the conversation drops off.

Don't take yourself and your efforts too seriously: Have fun and let your students have fun.

The chat exploration described above (while watching film in class) is fun for most (though not ALL) students. I try to experiment with 'fun' technologies several times during the term, most often soliciting ideas from students. But teachers have to have fun as well! Most of us feel guilty unless it's productive fun, so I suggest you set up something similar to our TWIT sessions (Teaching With Information Technologies) For years, we've held brown bag lunches at noon on Fridays. First we set up a name for the group that invited play. We made the explorations informative, "low overhead" in terms of preparation for the presenters, and fun. Have food and an informal, regular meeting time. Tap "experts" who have already used some system (email, word processing response tools, some aspect of the WWW, etc.) and after a very short presentation, have people use the system and play with it, exploring one thing and then another, learning from those around them. If someone has the energy, have them send out a short message describing what you all learned during the session for others who weren't able to come, thus sewing the seeds for your next session. Playful engagement is one of the primary survival skills for those trying to appropriately integrated communication technologies into classes.

Warning: Playful activities don't often convince administrators that important work is getting done, and you may be blessed with a "serious" administrator. None the less, at these informal meetings have a good time and then send out summaries of the event that focus on the "serious" work accomplished. The fun part will be spread by word of mouth soon enough.

Each time you engage in digital explorations use the PAR system: Preparation/Activity/Reflection.

I admit, it is tedious to think through the following questions before implementing any one technology-rich activity. But the method helps structure the planning of a technology-rich activity, and the questions quickly become second nature, part of your normal teaching procedure if they aren't already. Many teachers experienced with technologies would argue that you can over plan these activities and loose the spontaneity and value of the collaboration that might occur. I believe, however, that teachers new to any strange medium are uncertain about the value of the activities and, therefore, in need of a more structured approach to these online events. What follows is simply a list of questions to ask yourself as you prepare for an activity, as you engage that activity, and as you reflect on or use the materials that resulted from the event(s).

Preparation

> ‣ Is it clear to you and to others what is motivating the technology-rich event or activity?
> ‣ Are the likely outcomes of the online event explained to everyone?

▸ Do all participants have access to the necessary, working technology(ies)?

▸ Have you made it clear where and when the event will occur (In some cases, include time zones!)?

▸ Have you checked with technicians responsible for the system you will use and asked them or a support person to be available in case of emergencies?

▸ Do you have all the necessary documentation ready?

▸ If necessary have you conducted practice or training sessions with the participants ahead of time?

▸ Do you have a back-up plan if the system or activity is not working?

• Do participants know the etiquette guidelines you'd like them to follow when conversing online (see Appendix 1 for a sample)?

• If appropriate, have you sent out reminders to distant participants reminding them of where, when, and about what you will be meeting?

• Have you actually run through all the activities that you will be asking others to engage in?

Activity (During the Activity)

• Is your back-up plan ready to be implemented?

• Have you decided how or whether *you* will be participating and in what capacity?

• Do you have a method of "capturing" the session or session outcomes for the reflective events to follow? (If nothing else, have people freewrite on a piece of paper about the important moments, issues, or problems that came up immediately after the activity or event.)

• Are the support persons who will help people navigate and use the technologies present?

• Do you have email addresses or phone numbers of distant participants, if appropriate, in case there are technical problems during the online event?

Reflection

• How can you use the conversation or materials that resulted from the event?

- How can your students use the conversation?
- Can the conversation be useful to visitors? If so, how can you make it available to them in a form that they can actually use?
- If you've had an online conversation, have you asked the students to pick out the *gems* and *clinkers* of the conversation?

    Gems are the valuable ideas that surfaced.

    Clinkers are the half-baked ideas that need to be developed in more detail.
- Do you have some way of assessing whether the outcomes you expected were met or whether other unexpected outcomes resulted (for better or worse)?
- What revisions to the event/activity can you imagine? Write these down immediately!

Add a "critical component" to each lesson wherever possible.

English studies professionals generally do *not* want students to become habitual users and consumers of communication technologies per se. We do however introduce more students to these technologies than almost any other discipline and are implicated in the technological addictions that seem to be sprouting up around us. My "small potent gesture" (C. Selfe, 1999) in response to this trend is to encourage students to be critical, thoughtful users of these systems. I try to indicate the seriousness of my intent by building in to almost every use of technology some reflective or critical component.

All uses of technology have a critical edge to them, and we can, if we choose, integrate those edgy moments into our classes. I prefer to have critical, thoughtful, reflective sessions throughout the term instead of at any one point in the semester. Students get used to the rhythm of using technologies and then talking thoughtfully about how they might have influenced their learning, their working lives, or their personal lives. Eventually they begin coming up with critical issues of their own. Which is, of course, what we want.

Even the most ubiquitous communication technologies are ripe for critical analysis. Here are a few "for instances:"

TECHNOLOGY	CRITICAL COMPONENT(S)
e-mail	Talk about quoting with permission, privacy, or the over reliance or the avoidance of face-to-face interactions, . . .
Word processing	Talk about the ease of copying/nonattribution, appropriate uses of spell/grammar checking, commenting, and other tools, . . .
Web pages	Talk about intellectual property and plagiarism or the credibility of source materials, . . .
Scanning	Talk about copyright and fairuse doctrines, . . .
Synchronous environments (chatting)	Talk about civil exchanges, online communities, or the value/dangers of alternative online persona. . . .

Our job is to introduce these issues seamlessly into the activities and online events we create. Since all technology-rich activities are experimental by nature, the ethical and social issues that surround them are in flux as well. Each activity provides learning opportunities for us and our students during which we can thoughtfully explore current changing practices as well as the more traditional, often restrictive, institutional expectations that we all have to live with.

Network (in the interpersonal terms) with those around you: Some final strategies toward sustainable technology-rich instruction.

- *Talk to great teachers; get to know them, and then collaborate.*
  Read about, talk to, and listen carefully to people who seem to be excellent teachers: not just those who teach with technology, but anyone (in any discipline!) who seems to engage in interesting, productive teaching activities.

Some of the most interesting and productive idea sharing sessions that I've attended include people from a number of disciplines who are interested in communication activities. At Clemson University, for example, they have a formal Communication Across the Curriculum program. In their CAC alumni session (Spring 2001), I heard about some amazingly productive service learning approaches that involved faculty in the architecture and English departments and elementary school students and teachers (Sustainable School Yard projects). Those at institutions without formal CAC programs can draw people from around the institution by suggesting, holding, or attending informal communication technology sessions. How do you use effective class web pages? How can you "publish" student work? How do you use threaded discussions in class? The technology is the hook but the conversation should quickly turn to talk of pedagogy. Consider using the TWIT meetings (described above) to attract faculty and staff from across campus.

Collaborate locally if possible with teachers who have similar classes with similar objectives or with teachers with complementary course objectives (several such collaborations are detailed in the 1999 NCTE collection *Electronic Communication Across the Curriculum*). But also consider working with folks from a distance, even short distances (cross-town rivalries, for instance, are motivational and give students a reason to communicate with each other). Going to regional and national conferences and connecting with people gives you a chance to meet new folks and a excuse (which I always need) to go up and talk to presenters after a session. Once you get to know each other, imagine technology-mediated, cross-class, cross-institution units that will support both sets of class objectives.

- *At the end of each term, recruit students who are good at supporting others in their use of technology.*
  There is not much else to say here except that we need to develop a willingness to work with younger generations and to understand the nature of their literacy skills, experiences, and attitudes. This willingness seems to be a common characteristic of academics who are able to sustain their TWT activities over the years.

- *Share your insights.*
  Every time you conduct a techno-pedagogical exploration, whether it works or *not*, share your insights (formally, in presentations or publications or informally, in hallway conversations or over email lists like TechRhet < http://groups.yahoo. com/group /TechRhet/ >) with a community of scholar/teachers. We are all experimenting, all flailing about here in this changing educational world.

A conclusion?

There is no concluding this process. It's experimental; it changes; there are guidelines but few rules; there are many people who will continue to try to figure out where technology-rich and online systems are taking our first-year classes, pedagogies and curricula. If we connect with trusted others, and take slow, sustainable, reasoned steps into the swirling waters of technology-rich instruction, few will be swept away. See you in the shallow eddies.

Appendix 4.1

THE ECONOMY OF THE CCLI

INCOME

	number of people	fee/person	income
Lab fee for Majors	623	$215.00	$133,945.00
Lab fees for Non-Majors	71	$210.00	$14,910.00
Computer-Intensive Lab Fees: Service Courses	150	$45.00	$6,750.00
Computer-Intensive Lab Fees: STC Courses	190	$110.00	$20,900.00
CIWIC summer workshop fees	35	$50.00	$1,750.00
Other (e.g., summer consultant $, equip. sales)			$3,500.00

TOTAL YEARLY INCOME   **$181,755.00**

TOTAL INCOME   **$181,755.00**

SALARIES & WAGES

	# paid consultants	hours/ week	weeks/ year	hourly wage	salary totals
Lab consultant salaries: Academic year	6	9	50	$7.00	$18,900.00
Lab consultant salaries: Summer term	na	80	11	$7.00	$6,160.00
Systems Administrator	1	na	52	na	$44,000.00

TOTAL SALARY YEARLY EXPENSE   **$69,060.00**

HARDWARE EXPENSES

	#	cost/unit	initial cost	cost per year
Servers (replaced every 5 years)				
UNIX Servers (av. cost)	6	$10,000.00	$60,000.00	$12,000.00
Workstations (replaced every 3 years)				
Mac workstations	26	$1,800.00	$46,800.00	$15,600.00
Windows workstations	26	$1,500.00	$39,000.00	$13,000.00
kiosk with touch screen monitor	1	$2,000.00	$2,000.00	$666.67
Monitors (replaced every 3 years)	6	$300.00	$1,800.00	$600.00

TOTAL SERVER/WKSTATION YEARLY EXPENSE $41,866.67

	#	cost/unit	total cost	cost/year
Network Connectivity				
IT Phone Charges			$1,100.00	$1,100.00
IT Charges ($21.50/month=$258/year)	66	$258.00	$17,028.00	$17,028.00

TOTAL CONECTIVITY EXPENSE   **$18,128.00**

	#	cost/unit	total cost	cost/year
Printers & peripherals (replace every 3 years)				
Sun Monitor (bkup)	1	$400.00	$400.00	$133.33
SCSI card	1	$1,000.00	$1,000.00	$333.33
UPS backup system	6	$900.00	$5,400.00	$1,800.00
Sun tape backup	1	$4,000.00	$4,000.00	$1,333.33
backup tapes (replace each year)	6	$100.00	$600.00	$200.00
Diskpac	1	$15,000.00	$15,000.00	$5,000.00
CD Burner	2	$200.00	$400.00	$133.33
Desktop scanners	2	$350.00	$700.00	$233.33
Laserprinters	4	$2,700.00	$10,800.00	$3,600.00
Color printer	2	$1,200.00	$2,400.00	$800.00
Projection system	2	$5,000.00	$10,000.00	$3,333.33
Misc. cables			$300.00	$100.00
Miscellaneous costs (replaced every 1 year)				
Inkjet B&W & color cartridges	96	$27.00	$2,592.00	$2,592.00
Toner cartridges	36	$97.00	$3,492.00	$3,492.00
Zip drives	10	$100.00	$1,000.00	$1,000.00
CD-R (100/pack)	4	$80.00	$320.00	$320.00
Cleanup supplies			$300.00	$300.00
kiosk with touch screen monitor	1		$2,000.00	$2,000.00
Mice and Keyboards	20	$75.00	$1,500.00	$1,500.00

TOTAL YEARLY HARDWARE COST   **$26,204.00**

SOFTWARE EXPENSES

	#	unit cost	total cost	cost per year
for PC & Macintosh, Operating Systems (PC	25	$100.00	$2,500.00	$833.33
for PC & Macintosh, Operating Systems (MAC)	25	$125.00	$3,125.00	$1,041.67
all replaced/upgraded every 3 years, Page layout	50	$100.00	$5,000.00	$1,666.67
Security Software	1	$1,000.00	$1,000.00	$333.33
Drawing & Painting	50	$130.00	$6,500.00	$2,166.67
MS Office Suite	50	$100.00	$5,000.00	$1,666.67
Fonts	6	$200.00	$1,200.00	$400.00
Conferencing	2	$1,500.00	$3,000.00	$1,000.00
Multimedia Authoring	10	$600.00	$6,000.00	$2,000.00
3D Rendering	5	$250.00	$1,250.00	$416.67
Video Editing	2	$240.00	$480.00	$160.00
OCR	2	$400.00	$800.00	$266.67
Conversion (between platforms)	2	$200.00	$400.00	$133.33
Utilities	2	$120.00	$240.00	$80.00
Virus protection software	56	$30.00	$1,680.00	$560.00

TOTAL YEARLY SOFTWARE COSTS   **$12,725.00**

FURNITURE

	#	unit cost	total cost	cost per year
all amortized over 7 years surge protectors	15	$22.95	$344.25	$86.06
(except for surge protectors, workstation table	56	$500.00	$28,000.00	$4,000.00
replaced every 4 years) ergonomic chairs	56	$275.00	$15,400.00	$2,200.00
48" round table	1	$230.00	$230.00	$32.86
Storage cabinet (black)	2	$330.00	$660.00	$94.29
Table w/ locking casters	1	$200.00	$200.00	$28.57
Conference table	1	$500.00	$500.00	$71.43

TOTAL YEARLY FURNITURE COSTS   **$6,513.21**

TOTAL EXPENSES   **$174,496.87**

Appendix 5.1

ACCESS REDEFINED

The process description so far has, by necessity, stayed at a general level, and the outcomes may be hard imagine. The following is the kind of result that can emerge from sets of workshops of this type. The specifics came from the 1998 survey on the issue of access (D. Selfe, 1998). In the questionnaire, students, teachers, technicians, and administrators all helped defined what *access* meant to them at their institution. Compiling their insights proved to be both challenging and provocative.

Students and Access

If we want our students to thrive in electronic environments, do more than survive the technology-rich instruction we impose on them, we need to attend to the context of their learning situation. Several student respondents reframed the access issue in useful terms: They described it as *adequate time on appropriate workstations*. Others referred to access in terms of *student time*: the time students were able to make room in their hectic schedules to be where they needed to be to access appropriate environments. Several respondents mentioned the need for what I call adequate *"supported" work time*—time when human technical assistants were around to help troubleshoot difficult moments in the digital communication process. Add to this list the obvious need for *safe working environments* and the student definition of access becomes—adequate, safe, and supported work time on appropriate technology during manageable periods of time relative to the students' own schedules and responsibilities.

Teachers and Access

Teachers had unique needs of course. In addition to the adequate, safe, and supported work time on appropriate technology that the students requested, teachers—even enthusiastic technology advocates—often saw technology development as an additional burden added to a substantial content-filled curriculum. Because of that perspective, they wanted *rhetorically situated workshops* focused not just on the technologies—"Today we are going to learn how to use the (Style) option in Microsoft Word"—but technology instruction and demonstrations that could be made relevant to the teaching and administrative projects they already had underway ("At the end of my advanced composition course, I need to illustrate to students quickly and efficiently how different designs of their written projects can influence the way a reader responds to the project. To accomplish this in one class session, I teach them how to use the "Style" option in Microsoft Word.") Teachers also identified *points in the technology-integration effort when human support for their projects became critical* while:

- learning the technologies,
- planning to integrate those technologies into their classes,
- implementing technology-rich instruction in their classes, online, and in campus facilities, and finally
- reassessing the value of technology-rich instruction and investigating more effective uses of new technologies.

Technicians and Access

If we are going to work toward providing the kind of sophisticated access defined earlier (and it will take concerted, long-term efforts to do so), we need to become/remain aware of the forces acting on technical support people. Access for technicians can mean a number of things:

- the number of hours of secure access when machines and peripherals won't disappear: *security*
- the number of hours of "supported" work time that can be provided: time when *paid or volunteer consultants* were available to users
- some amount of *controlled access* where all users are authenticated

- the ability to *distribute the load on the system* so that no one moment will bring the network to its knees (e.g., as a class all logs in at once and fires up network hogging applications)
- the *speed* of workstations that need to accommodate more and more complex media projects
- the ability to identify *bottlenecks* in the full educational cycle: from delivering assignments; to licensing software; to providing storage space, to providing input devices (scanners) and appropriate workstations; to maintaining network speed and providing appropriate output devices for students' and teachers' projects: the WWW, gray-scale and color printers, network publishing systems, CD presses

Access is a complex business to technical support folks. It grows more difficult as English studies professionals succeed in our efforts to integrate technologies into our curricula. As you can tell, those efforts are expensive. All of these come with a price tag, and technical support people, in all but rare occasions, have to work within constraining budgets that are often outside their control.

Local Administrators and Access

Those stakeholders with apparent control of technology budgets are local academic administrators. Unfortunately, these administrators often have limited discretionary funds at their disposal and, at the same time, are asked by upper administrators to justify their computing expenses based on rather simplistic formulas. Adequate access to technology, for instance, might be defined by upper administrators as simply the number of students/seat: the number, at Michigan Tech., for instance, is set at around 10 students to every workstation. Compared to students', teachers', and technicians' notions of access (the real demands that local administrators hear), this type of definition seems fairly inadequate and certainly does not address the perceived needs of other stakeholders.

In addition to mediating between simplistic assumptions about technological access coming from above and the detailed and immediate access needs of students, faculty, and staff, most local administrators face a complex of unique access issues. They think or should be thinking about the department's or program's ability to provide appropriate access to digital technologies over time. For an administrator, then, sustained access for their department includes:

- an *amortized budget* (for physical facilities) that break down roughly this way:[1]
  45%   salaries and wages
  30%   hardware
  20%   software
   5%   expendables
- the constant struggle to *hire or retain support personnel* who are in great demand locally and in industry and who may draw salaries that exceed those of the professors they work with
- attempts to *retain, tenure, and promote faculty* who use new, innovative technologies in their classes and as a result often have atypical research and teaching profiles
- the effort to *supply and train faculty* on new communication technologies in a systematic fashion
- an *assessment model* that evaluates both the instruction that goes on in technology-rich environments and the environments themselves.

Some of these access-related issues may seem distant and tangential, at first glance, to the process of having students log into a technology-rich environment or of having them connect to a wide-area network to complete the assignments for literacy professionals. Yet these issues all have rather important and direct consequences for each of the stakeholders in new technology-rich environments. Safety issues can inhibit even the most dedicated returning student from attempting and completing assignments. A system without reliable backups can result in the loss of weeks, even months, of work by teachers and students. Short-term financial plans will produce technology environments that quickly become dated and unusable for students and teachers alike.

The following are some examples of the action items developed in response to the *access* issue as it was redefined here. We have attempted to apply these action items in the CCLI in the Humanities department at MTU.

---

[1]The figures we calculated from the combined budgets submitted in the 1996 survey of technology-rich facilities. For a more complete description of how they were calculated, see Selfe (1997). These figures can serve as a rough guideline for those interested in strategic planning for classrooms, labs, and centers. Of course the ongoing costs of online environments would radically change these percentages.

Access from the Students' Perspective

A program might work to provide
- *safe & supported access*—Staff the facility or environment with knowledgeable consultants for 100 hours per week in order to maintain a safe, well supported learning environment. (These consultants can be either physically or virtually present depending on the nature of the technology-rich instruction.)
- *adequate student work time*—Abide by the 20%/80% principle: 20% class-time access and 80% work-time access on the same or equivalent workstations. In a lab or classroom that provides both instructional time and independent work time, this translation is simple. 20% of the time can be used for class instruction while the rest is used for open work hours. On campuses where open labs are maintained, students should be able to access similar, at least equivalent machines 3-4 hours for every computer-intensive class hour. The same can be said for or online work environments, where providing adequate access is essential and may be part of a list of pre-requisites for the class.
- *adequate workstations*—Provide a predictable amortized budget that enables the technical staff to upgrade software and hard-ware on a *reasonable*, though not necessarily cutting edge, timetable.

Access for Teachers

A program might work to provide
- *consistent professional development opportunities*—Make avail-able a number of convenient venues for professional develop-ment opportunities on a weekly, term-by-term, and yearly basis.
- *desk-side assistance*—Recruit, train, and pay student technolo-gy assistants to support faculty and staff working on technolo-gy-rich projects.
- *support efforts to evaluate those teaching with technology*—Hold end-of-term show-and-tell sessions with a formative evaluation component built in. Have teachers ask themselves and their students questions like these: What technology-rich activities did you try? How did they work? What will you do to improve them?

Access for Technicians

A program might work to provide
- *secure, convenient access to technology*—Set up human, hardware, and software security systems without unnecessarily encumbering the working activities of students and teachers.
- *adequate hardware, software, and network conditions*—Monitor the actual, useable speed requirements and levels of frustration of students and teachers as they work on the systems.
- *an appropriate budget*—Lobby for a revenue stream capable of avoiding systemic bottlenecks in technology-rich instructional processes.

Access for Administrators

A program might work to provide
- *recruitment and professional development procedures*—Provide a flexible tenure and promotion procedure that encourages appropriate, though always risky technology-rich instructional innovation.
- *reasonable support from outside the department*—Educate upper administrators about the "real" costs of technology-rich innovation in human, technical, and financial terms.

Appendix 5.2

TEACHING WITH INFORMATION TECHNOLOGY (TWIT)

This e-mail outlines the type of sessions we planned for, as a group, early in the 1999–2000 school year. The items mentioned and the activities suggested are not dissimilar from those that occur today or those that we held in the early 1990s. The humor, informality, and low-key nature of these meetings are also revealed in Danielle's notes from this planning session (Danielle DeVoss is now a faculty member in the graduate department at Michigan State University).

To: rselfe@mtu.edu
From: Danielle DeVoss <dndevoss@mtu.edu>
Subject: twitnotes
NOTES FROM TWIT —where we're headed this year
September 3, 1999
****
DICKIE'S OBJECTIVES:

1. more sessions connecting with people off campus (via MOO, RealVideo, etc.)
2. to get a better sense of what's available on all sorts of different systems and in use at different places
   (possible 3: combine both objectives—chatting with people using different systems)
****
GENERAL IDEAS:

- session for new folks: resources, organizations, groups, conferences, email lists, etc. on teaching with technology

- planning Computers and Writing proposals/abstracts (deadline: late October; conference date: late May in Fort Worth, TX)
- technology-related jobs: looking at ads, finding out what's out there, situating yourself in correspondence and discussions, finding out what you'll be asked when you're out there
- using/maintaining 134 (e.g., how to run projection, how to use audio, how to twist arms to get air conditioning, how to work on better acoustics in the room, etc.)
- integrating technology into our teaching—HU101T, HU101H, HU333
- theory smorgasbord/"my favorite theory"/it's a big field out there: the complexities and multiplicities of teaching with technology (depth and breadth and sorting things out)
- toy smorgasbord: sharing our favorite stuff to use
- grants: what sources are available, how to find them, how to approach money-givers, hints and tips on writing grants
- questions and answers with techies: talking to our system administrator and the CCLI consultants
- new purchases/how to better use what we have (e.g., mobile projection systems in the CCLI and in classrooms, digital camera, etc.)
- more on communicating at a distance in general
- the tattoos of technical people: who's got 'em and what they're of ;)

****

ANALYSIS OF ONLINE CLASS SYSTEMS:

- testing of/talking about HU Web class set up on WebCT (new this year through the university); e.g., how to better connect/route around built-in firewalls
- explore Syllaweb, Syllabase, SITES and other online course software/development tools (University of Utah, Texas Tech and others are using—they might give us access to test classes)

REFERENCES

Brown, J.S., & Duguid, P. (2000). *The social life of information*. Boston: Harvard Business School Press.

Bruce, B., Peyton, J.K., & Batson, T. (Ed.). (1993). *Network-based classrooms: Promises and realities*. Cambridge: Cambridge University Press.

Certeau, M.D. (1984). *The practice of everyday life* (S. Randall, Trans.). Berkeley: University of California Press.

Coffield, K., Essid, J., Lasarenko, J., Record, L., Selfe, D., & Stilley, H. (2000). Surveying the virtual terrain: A guide to forming a supportive teaching community. In R. Rickley, S. Harrington, & M. Day (Eds.), The online writing classroom (pp. 285-317). Cresskill, NJ: Hampton Press.

Coley, R.J., Crandler, J., & Engle, P. (1997). *Computers and classrooms: The status of technology in U.S. schools*. Princeton, NJ: Educational Testing Service.

Collard, A. (1987). *Rape of the wild*. Bloomington: Indiana University Press.

DeVoss, D., Hayden, D., Selfe, C., & Selfe, R. (2001). Distance education: Sites of political agency. In E.E. Schell & P.L. Stock (Eds.), *Moving a mountain* (pp. 261-286). Urbana, IL: NCTE.

Ellul, J. (1964). *The technological society* (J. Wilkinson, Trans.). New York: Vintage.

Faigley, L. (1992). The achieved utopia of the networked classroom. In *Fragments of rationality: Postmodernity and the subject of composition* (pp. 163–199). Pittsburgh: University of Pittsburgh Press.

Feenberg, A. (1991). *Critical theory of technology*. New York: Oxford University Press.

Feenberg, A. (1995). *Alternative modernity: The technical turn in philosophy and social theory*. Berkeley: University of California Press.

Feenberg, A., & Hannay, A. (Eds.). (1995). *Technology & the politics of knowledge*. Bloomington: Indiana University Press.

Getting America's Students Ready for the 21st Century: Meeting the Technology Literacy Challenge, A Report to the Nation on Technology and Education. (1996). Report from the U.S. Department of Education, Washington, DC.

Giddens, A. (1979). *Central problems in social theory: Action, structure and contradiction in social analysis*. Berkeley: University of California Press.

Gilbert, S. (1997, January 9). Talk delivered at The Epiphany Project Institute, *Astride the divide: Mapping new rhetorical spaces in the teaching of composition.* Washington, DC: George Mason University.

Gilbert, S. (1995, March/April). Teaching, learning, and technology: The need for campus-wide planning and faculty support services. *Change,* pp. 47–52.

Green, K.C. (1997). The campus computing project (November 1996): The national survey of information technology in higher education [On-line]. *AskERIC.* Available: < http://ericir.syr.edu/Projects/Campus_computing > .

Green, K.C., & Gilbert, S.W. (1995, March/April). Content, communications, productivity, and the role of information technology in higher education. *Change,* pp. 8–19.

Hawisher, G.E., & Selfe, C. (1993). Tradition and change in computer-supported writing environments: A call for action. In P. Kahaney, J. Janangelo, & L.A.M. Perry (Eds.), *Theoretical and critical perspectives on teacher change* (pp. 155–186). Norwood, NJ: Ablex.

HR 1804, Goals 2000: Educate America Act. March 31, 1994, < http://www.ed.gov//legislation/GOALS20000/TheAct > .

IEEE Transactions on Professional Communication. (December 1996). *39*(4).

Johnson, R. (1998). *User-centered technology: A rhetorical theory for computers and other mundane artifacts.* Albany: State University of New York Press.

Kemp, F. (2000). Surviving in English departments: The stealth computer-based writing program. In R. Rickly, S. Harrington, & M. Day (Eds.), *The on-line writing classroom* (pp. 267–284). Cresskill, NJ: Hampton Press.

Landauer, T.K. (1995). *The trouble with computers: Usefulness, usability, and productivity.* Cambridge, MA: MIT Press.

Latour, B. (1996). *ARAMIS or the love of technology* (C. Porter, Trans.). Cambridge, MA: Harvard University Press.

Lave, J., & Wegner, E. (1993). *Situated learning: Legitimate peripheral participation.* New York: Cambridge University Press.

LeBlanc, P. (1995). Finding our place on the Infobahn: A report from the corporate research lab. Paper delivered at Conference on College Composition and Communication, Washington, DC.

Mead, M. (1970). *Culture and commitment: A study of the generation gap.* Garden City, NY: Natural History Press/Doubleday.

Michigan Curriculum Framework: Content Standards and Benchmarks. (1995). Lansing: Michigan Department of Education.

Moran, C., & Selfe, C. (1998). *Access to technology and the wealth gap in America.* Unpublished manuscript.

Nardi, B.A., & O'Day, V. (1999). *Information ecologies: Using technology with heart.* Cambridge, MA: MIT Press.

Norman, D. (1989). *The design of everyday things.* Cambridge, MA: MIT Press.

Reiss, D., Selfe, R., & Young, A. (Eds.). (1998). *Electronic communication across the curriculum.* Urbana, IL: NCTE.

Selfe, C. (1989a). *Creating a computer-supported writing facility: A blueprint for action.* West Lafayette, IN: Computers and Composition Press.

Selfe, C. (1989b). Multilayered grammars of literacy. In Gail Hawisher & C. Selfe (Eds.), *Critical perspectives on computers and composition studies* (pp. 3–15). New York: Teachers College Press.

Selfe, C. (1999). *Technology and literacy in the twenty-first century: The importance of paying attention.* Carbondale: Southern Illinois University Press.

Selfe, C., & Hilligoss, S. (Eds.). (1994). *Literacy and computers: The complications of teaching and learning with technology.* New York: MLA.

Selfe, C., & Selfe, D. (1994). The politics of the interface. *College Composition and Communication, 45*(4), 480-504.

Selfe, C., & Selfe, D. (1995). Writing as democratic social action in a technological world: Politicizing and inhabiting virtual landscapes. In A. Duin-Hill & C. Hansen (Eds.), *Nonacademic writing: Social theory and technology* (pp. 325–358). Hillsdale, NJ: Lawrence Erlbaum Associates.

Selfe, D. (1995a). *Surviving the journey: Practical strategies for computers & writing program development.* Workshop presentation at Computers and Writing Conference, El Paso, TX.

Selfe, D. (1995b). Surfing the tsunami: Electronic environments in the writing center. *Computers and Composition, 12*(3), 311–322.

Selfe, R. (1998). *The instructional, technical, and institutional challenges of supporting technology-rich communication facilities.* Unpublished dissertation, Michigan Technological University.

Selfe, D. (2003). Techno-pedagogical explorations: Toward sustainable technology-rich instruction. In P. Takayoski & B. Huot (Eds.), *Teaching writing with computers: An introduction* (pp. 17–32). Boston: Houghton Mifflin.

Standards for the English Language Arts. (1996). Newark, DE, and Urbana, IL: International Reading Association and the National Council of Teachers of English.

The Condition of Education 1997. (1997). U.S. Department of Education, National Center for Education Statistics, Washington, DC: U.S. Government Printing Office, NCES 97-388.

The Condition of Education 1998. (June 1998). U.S. Department of Education, National Center for Education Statistics,. Washington, DC: U.S. Government Printing Office, NCES 98-013.

Wahlstrom, B., & Selfe, C. (1992). A view from the bridge: English departments piloting among the shoals of computer use. *ADE Bulletin, 109,* 35–45.

Williams, S. (2002, Summer). Why are partnerships necessary for computer classroom administration? *Technical Communication Quarterly, 11*(3), 339–358.

Zuboff, S. (1988). *In the age of the smart machine: The future of work and power.* New York: Basic.

AUTHOR INDEX

B

Brown, J.S., 57, 150, *179*
Bruce, B., xii, xx, 79, *179*

C

Coffield, K., 106, 115, *179*
Coley, R.J., 3, *179*
Crandler, J., 3, *179*

C

DeVoss, D., 153, *179*
Duguid, P., xii, xx, 57, 150, *179*

E

Engle, P., 3, *179*
Essid, J., 106, 115, *179*

F

Feenberg, A., xviii, 153, *179*

G

Giddens, A., 54, *179*
Gilbert, S., 87, 109, *180*
Green, K.C., 3, *180*

H

Hannay, A., 153, *179*

Hayden, D., 153, *179*
Hawisher, G.E., 8, *180*

J

Johnson, R., xviii, 49, *180*

K

Kemp, F., 13, 15, 17, *180*

L

Landauer, T.K., 16($n2$), *180*
Lasarenko, J., 106, 115, *179*
Lave, J., 150, *180*
LeBlanc, P., 151, *180*

M

Mead, M., 88, *180*
Moran, C., 55, *180*

N

Nardi, B.A., 55, *180*
Norman, D., 58, *180*

O

O'Day, V., 55, *180*

R

Reiss, D., 15, *180*

S

Selfe, C., 2, 8, 14, 33 44, 153, 161,
    179, 180, 181
Selfe, D., x, 8, 106, 115, *181*
Selfe, R., 8, 15, 108, 153, 153(*n*1),
    181

W

Wegner, E., 150, *180*
Williams, S., 106, *181*

Y

Young, A., 15, *180*

SUBJECT INDEX

A

access (accessibility), 2, 4, 8, 19, 25, 33, 43-45, 48, 58, 67, 69-70, 75, 89, 93-94, 96-97, 104. 108, 132, 135-136, 144, 146, 171, 176

achievement, 4, 40

activist (activism, technological activism, 120, 135, 142, 146

administrator, 1, 4, 8-10, 13, 27-28, 32, 34, 37-38 42-43, 58-59, 66-67, 69, 76, 86, 90, 104-107, 109-110, 122-123, 126-127, 133, 142-144, 146

afford (affordance), 8, 13, 58

assessment (formative, assess), 8, 21, 25, 28, 37, 42, 48, 59, 65, 86, 91, 96, 103, 120, 121-128, 131-137, 141-143, 146-147

B

Ball State University

Baltimore City College High School, 99-102

Bread Loaf (BreadNet), xiii, xv, xvi, xvii, xviii

Brown University, 38-40

C

Center for Computer-Assisted Language Instruction (CCLI), 55-57, 62-69, 87-90, 94-95, 104, 106-107, 117-118, 124, 131-133, 135-137, 141

Cincinnati State Technical College (2-year college), 105

Clemson University, 111-112

collaborate (collaboration, collaborating, collaboratively), 6, 18, 25, 36, 48, 62-63, 69, 74-77, 84, 93, 97, 104, 117, 128, 144

college (university, higher education), 3, 18, 37, 45, 47, 55, 64-65, 69-70, 72, 82, 87, 94-95, 102-106, 110-112, 117-119, 128-129, 138-139

Colorado State University, 50-51

compose, 6, 14, 44, 60, 104, 128, 138-139

computer-supported (see also technology-rich teaching), 7-9, 11, 14, 24-25, 27, 29, 34, 36, 41-43, 47-48, 54-56, 58-59, 60, 64, 67, 69, 71, 74, 76, 82, 85, 88, 90-96, 106-107, 109, 111-112, 116-120, 121-122, 123, 126-128, 133, 135-137, 142-147

cyborg, 15, 55-58, 82, 122-123

D

database-driven systems (web-based systems), 80, 115, 128-129

design (*See* re-design)

digital literacy (technological literacy), 5, 17, 37, 89, 116, 138

distance education (distributed education, online instruction), 25, 38, 72-73, 75, 128, 142, 144

dynamic of blame (DOB), 1, 8-12, 24-25, 41, 87, 108, 146

E

800-Pound Gorilla, 81-83, 85

ecology (information ecology), 55, 122

entrepreneur (entrepreneurial), 85, 110-115

experiment (experimental, experimentation, exploratory), 19, 25, 42, 55, 72, 75, 88, 107

F

face-to-face (F2F), 19, 67, 69, 75, 93, 96

financial (finance, fiscal, budget), 9, 23, 27, 32, 58, 65, 67, 69-70, 74, 81-82, 85-86, 91, 94, 96, 105-111, 116, 118-120, 122, 132, 138, 141, 165-169

G

grant, 24, 35, 50, 65, 77, 85, 115-119

I

infrastructure, 7-8, 37, 45, 57, 86, 117-118

integration, 41, 69, 73, 87, 97, 106, 128-129, 139

instructional needs (pedagogical needs or goals), 54, 59-60, 63-64, 66-67, 69-71, 74, 76, 81, 85, 87-91, 103, 106-107, 116, 119, 122, 124, 132, 135, 137-138, 144-146

involvement (intervention) 8, 28, 42, 44-45, 49, 89, 91-92, 94-96, 107, 118, 120, 121, 124, 133-137, 141-144, 146

J

James Madison University, 113-115

K

K-12 (K-12 institutions, K-college), 36, 45, 62, 64, 82, 87, 90-91, 95-97, 111, 117, 119, 127, 138, 142

L

lab fee, 85, 94, 107, 110, 118-119

literacy (instruction, needs, practices, professionals, specialists, skills), 1-3, 6-14, 16-18, 23-28, 33-34, 36-38, 41-42, 44, 49, 58, 60-62, 64, 69, 71-72, 74, 76-77, 81, 88-89, 91, 95-96, 105, 107, 110-112, 116, 119, 122, 136, 146-147

M

matrix, 125, 131, 133-137, 141

Michigan Technological University

(MTU), 15, 46-47, 64-66, 88, 104, 107, 109, 117-119, 124, 127, 132, 135-136, 141

N

Northern Illinois University, 137-140

O

operational (operational goals, operationalize), 14-16, 54, 59, 63-64, 66-71, 74-76, 81, 87, 89-90, 106, 119

online (databases, games, venues, environments; virtual), 1, 14-15, 17, 25, 28-29, 36, 42-44, 47-48, 56, 67, 69-70, 72-75, 81-82, 90, 94-97, 106-109, 111-112, 116-117, 127, 132, 142

overdetermined, 12

P

Penn State University, 72-73

people, first (people first, pedagogy second, technology third), 1, 12, 14, 105

planning process, 14, 18, 54, 62, 64

Portland Middle School, 97-99

position of strength, 16, 53, 59, 69

professional development, 4, 7-8, 11-12, 26, 29, 33, 44-45, 48, 63, 67, 69, 86, 113, 132

R

re-design (design, ongoing design, redesigned, designers), 14-15, 17-18, 34, 36-37, 41, 45-49, 53-54, 57-60, 62, 67, 69-71, 74-77, 81-82, 86, 88, 91-92, 94-96, 99, 106-107, 111-112, 117, 119-120, 121-127, 131-137, 141-142, 144-147

S

self directed (self supporting, self-determining), 47, 57, 64, 91, 101. 130

staff (technical, technicians), 8, 10-11, 13, 15, 34-37, 42-45, 54, 57, 63, 66-67, 69-71, 74, 76, 86, 89-90, 92-93, 97, 104, 107, 109-111, 116-120, 122-123, 127, 133, 135, 142

stakeholder (stakeholder-centered), 54, 66-67, 69, 71,74, 76-77, 82, 87, 90, 92. 105-107, 110, 120-127, 132-133, 135-137, 141-143, 146-147

standards (goals, benchmarks), 4-5, 8, 27-28, 34, 39, 44, 87, 89-90, 94, 105-106, 130, 135, 137-138, 147

student technology assistant (pro-grams), 45-46, 85, 87,88, 90, 92-95, 97, 102-105, 120

support crisis, 109

sustain (sustainable, sustainable practices), 13, 15, 23-24, 26-28, 33-34, 37-38, 41-43, 49, 55-56, 58-59, 81, 85-87, 90-92, 96, 99, 104-107, 110-112, 116, 118, 120, 122-123, 128, 132-133, 135, 137-138, 141-142, 146-147

T

technical communication, 65, 72, 89, 105, 111, 122, 127

technology-rich teaching (instruc-tion, literacy instruction, instruc-tional systems, labs, classrooms, virtual systems), 23, 25-27, 29, 33, 36-38, 41-43, 45-49, 53-56, 58, 62, 64, 69, 74, 77, 81-82, 86,

91, 93-94, 104, 120, 121, 126, 128, 137, 142

techno-pedagogical, 27-28, 153-164

tenure, 21, 25, 29, 32, 37, 42, 112, 142

Texas Tech University, 29, 48

TWIT (teaching with information technology), 177-178

U

ubiquitous, 3, 15, 138

underdetermined, 147

university (*See* college)

University of Texas at Austin, 30-32, 48

University of Utah, 128-131

user-centered, 49, 53, 58, 70, 74-75, 81, 124

W

West Noble High School, 34-36

William Patterson University, 103-104

X

XML (*See* database-driven)